What Research Says to the Science Teacher

Volume Five

Problem Solving

Dorothy Gabel, editor

National Science Teachers Association

Volume 5
What Research Says to the Science Teacher
Problem Solving

pub. 6,38
7/19/90

This book has been edited and produced by the staff of Special Publications, the National Science Teachers Association, 1742 Connecticut Avenue, N.W. Washington, D.C. 20009. Phyllis R. Marcuccio, Director of Publications; Shirley Watt Ireton, Managing Editor of Special Publications; Deborah C. Fort, Free-lance Editor; Michael Shackleford, Assistant Editor; Cheryle L. Shaffer, Assistant Editor.

Library of Congress Catalog Card Number 89-062358
ISBN Number 0-87355-084-6

Printed in the United States of America
First edition

Introduction

Any attempt to synthesize the research on problem solving in science is an ambitious undertaking. Part of the problem lies in the very definition of problem solving. There is a wide spectrum of definitions, some very broad, others quite narrow. How does problem solving differ from critical thinking, inquiry learning, and/or process skills, particularly at the integrated level? And is the addition of 15 + 23 really an arithmetic *problem?* Many would call this solving an *exercise.* Perhaps it is best to think of the definitions of problem solving as being on a continuum. At one end are problems to which no one has the answer such as "What is the cure for AIDS?" At the other are exercises whose solutions are known to most adults (such as 15 + 23 = 38) but not to a child whose reasoning power is beginning to develop. In other words, a problem for one person may not be a problem for another person who readily understands the pathway to its solution.

No effort has been made here to resolve the question of how a problem is defined; neither, however, do we sidestep it. In the chapters on problem solving at the elementary and middle school levels, Betty J. McKnight and Stanley L. Helgeson take an approach through process skills. In the chapter on Earth sciences, Charles R. Ault, Jr., concentrates on solving global qualitative problems. Mike U. Smith's chapter on biology, Ray M. Snider's on physics, and mine on chemistry focus more on mathematical problem solving. The definition of problem solving adopted by various authors determined which research they reviewed and, consequently, shaped the thrust of their papers. Donald Robert Woods, however, includes a number of definitions of the concept in his paper on helpful problem-solving practices.

A question of greater importance for teachers than the definition of a problem is the question of why problem solving is included in the science classroom. Teachers assign problems that experts might consider exercises to help students learn concepts. These same problems (or slight variations thereon) are included on tests to determine whether students understand the concepts on which the problems are based. Students, however, are clever and are frequently able to solve such problems without understanding the underlying concepts. The students have memorized algorithms that bypass thinking but produce correct answers. Having students solve problems for which answers are already known and which experts would generally view as exercises Paul F. Brandwein (1971) calls "problem doing" rather than "problem solving."

Many teachers include *real* problem solving in their courses because they feel that this activity teaches students to act as scientists. If this is the purpose of including problem solving in the curriculum, then problems must be more than exercises. Brandwein elucidates the scientist's role in problem solving:

> Does a scientist, then, ever engage in "problem solving"? Of course [s/]he does, as part of an investigation; but the *elaboration of the problem* is part of a strategy for solving the problem; the *statement* of the problem is but one tactic. This deserves further clarification. I wish we did not require a schema of the scientist's art of investigation; being an art, it defies description: It is idiosyncratic; it is creative. Nevertheless, for our present purposes, we may try to plot the general area of the scientist's way—his[/her] methods of intelligence. (pp.19-20)*

---

*From *Substance, Structure, and Style in the Teaching of Science—New Edition,* by Paul F. Brandwein, copyright© 1971, 1968, 1965 Harcourt Brace Jovanovich, Inc.

A Diagram of a Scientist's Way: *methods of intelligence*

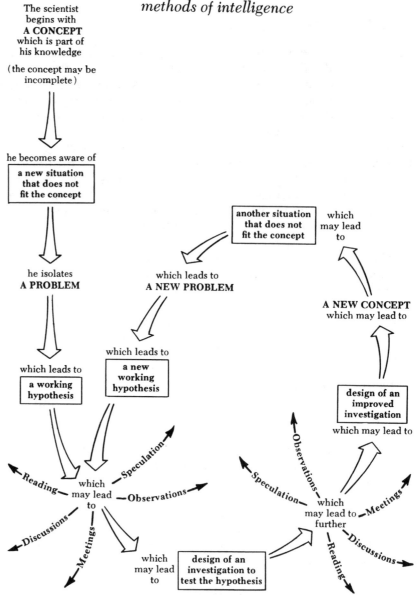

The scientist begins with **A CONCEPT** which is part of his knowledge

(the concept may be incomplete)

he becomes aware of

a new situation that does not fit the concept

he isolates **A PROBLEM**

which leads to **a working hypothesis**

which may lead to —Reading— —Speculation— —Observations— —Discussions— —Meetings—

which may lead to **design of an investigation to test the hypothesis**

which leads to **a new working hypothesis**

which leads to **A NEW PROBLEM**

another situation that does not fit the concept

which may lead to

A NEW CONCEPT which may lead to

design of an improved investigation

which may lead to

which may lead to further —Speculation— —Observations— —Meetings— —Discussions— —Reading—

Brandwein describes the scientist's method of intelligence (as depicted above) as follows:

> The brief, oversimplified scheme emphasizes the poverty of *steps* in a "scientific method"; the essence of the scientist's way (call it inquiry if you must) is an art which calls upon the bright luminosity of . . . imagination as well as the sober processes in the library, laboratory, and the conference room. But the sea of science is essentially an individual's mind, not the laboratory. (p. 22)

This approach to problem solving is a far cry from what occurs in most science classrooms. If one of the objectives of science education is to have students become problem solvers because this is the activity of scientists, then the present activities that occur in the science classroom under the guise of "problem solving" must change dramatically to become much more based on inquiry.

A final word to the readers of this volume. Although much research has been done on problem solving, many questions remain unanswered. The research across the various disciplines in science is uneven. Research on problem solving in each field has not progressed to the same point. For example, more research has been done on physics problem solving than on chemistry, biology, and Earth science. Although each discipline has its own peculiarities, findings in one often provide insights about problem solving in another. For this reason, a teacher of chemistry should not restrict him/herself to reading only the chapter on chemistry. What Smith has to say about biology students' successful and unsuccessful approaches to solving problems in genetics may well apply to chemistry students working on stoichiometry problems.

Similarities about research findings and implications for teaching also exist across the chapters of this book even though I made no attempt to ask authors to follow outlines. For example, most authors discuss the importance of conceptual understanding, the role of misconceptions, and the use of pattern recognition, heuristics, and algorithms in problem solving. Almost all advocate a hands-on approach to the teaching of science. All are concerned with problem solving as a means to promote student understanding rather than as merely a means of obtaining correct solutions. These recurring themes give credence to some commonalities about problem solving across the disciplines, principles that may have wide classroom applications.

All the authors hope that science teachers will be able to incorporate at least some of these findings on problem solving into their classrooms. After all, we translated problem-solving research into practice to give teachers new insights into helping students become better problem solvers.

Dorothy L. Gabel
Fall, 1989

Reference

Brandwein, Paul F. (1971). *Substance, structure, and style in the teaching of science.* New York: Harcourt Brace Jovanovich.

Charles R. Ault, Jr. Currently an associate professor in Lewis and Clark College's department of education where he teaches both elementary and secondary education courses, Ault received his A.B. from Dartmouth College in 1972 and his Ph.D. from Cornell University in 1980. His scholarly interests include the development of basic science concepts in both children and adults, interview protocols in research about science misconceptions, and evaluation of visitors' interpretations of science museum exhibits. He is working on evaluation studies of visitor interpretations of the "Superheroes: A High Tech Adventure" exhibit at the Oregon Museum of Science and Industry.

Dorothy L. Gabel. A former high school chemistry teacher, Gabel received her Ph.D. from Purdue University and now teaches science education at Indiana University. She is the author of a text on problem solving for high school chemistry students and coauthor of *Chemistry: The Study of Matter.* She has presented workshops on chemistry problem solving throughout the country, chaired the NSTA Task Force on Problem Solving from 1981–1983, and was the NSTA Research Division Director from 1983–1985. Currently she is directing an NSF-supported project, which is producing videotapes on exemplary chemistry teaching.

Stanley L. Helgeson. At Ohio State University, Helgeson is professor of science education and associate director for science education of the ERIC Clearinghouse for Science, Mathematics, and Environmental Education. He is especially interested in problem solving, concept learning, evaluation, and the applications of microcomputers to science teaching. In the past he has served as president of the National Association for Research in Science Teaching and as a member of the research committee and executive board of the NSTA.

Betty J. McKnight. Professor emeritus of science education, McKnight is a recipient of the New York State Chancellor's Award for Excellence in College Teaching. She is coauthor of seven elementary science textbooks and has taught science at all levels. From 1971 until her retirement in 1988, she taught at the College at New Paltz of the State University of New York. Since receiving her Ph.D. in science education from Cornell University, she has written, done research, and consulted in learning theory and curriculum development.

Mike U. Smith. At the Mercer University School of Medicine, Smith is associate professor of medical education. Smith received his B.S. in genetics from Union University, his M.S. from Purdue University in molecular genetics, and his Ph.D. from Florida State University in science education. A member of the editorial board of the *Journal of Research in Science Teaching,* Smith's research has focused on problem solving, instruction, and artificial intelligence.

Ray M. Snider. Professor of science education and chair of the department of secondary education at the College at New Paltz of the State University of New York, Snider teaches graduate classes in educational measurement and evaluation and undergraduate and graduate classes in science teaching methods and curriculum. With a B.S. from the State University of New York (Albany), an M.S. from Rensselaer Polytechnic Institute, and a Ph.D. in science education from Cornell University, Snider has taught students at secondary, undergraduate, and graduate levels.

Donald Robert Woods. Director of the engineering and management program and former chair of the department of chemical engineering, Woods has presented over 200 workshops to educators and industrialists worldwide on the development of problem-solving skills. Over the past 20 years, he has developed a four-course sequence of required courses to develop interpersonal and problem-solving skills. Since 1983, Woods has been writing "PS Corner," a column in *Journal of College Science Teaching;* since 1979, he has been the author of *PS News,* a news letter.

Problem Solving in Elementary School Science

Betty J. McKnight
The College at New Paltz
State University of New York

Problem-solving skills should develop on a firm foundation built by each child's earliest experiences. The difficulty high school and college teachers encounter in teaching problem solving strongly suggests that most students' early education does not create this ideal foundation. What does research suggest to the teacher of young children?

Before a student can solve a problem, he or she must recognize that there is a problem to be solved. If teachers can introduce experiences that make students aware of discrepancies between what they expect and what they observe, students will learn to ask questions. Questioning will help students to define and ultimately to solve problems.

Such experiences can be both spontaneous events and teacher-planned activities. The natural world offers an inexhaustible supply of experiences for students: experiences that will add to general knowledge, stimulate curiosity, create a need to know. If young students are given hands-on experience with materials, they develop better language skills and better concepts of form—both of which lead to better problem-solving skills.

Discrepancies—differences, inconsistencies, disagreements, disharmonies—can only be perceived by comparison with prior experience. Since some children have had more experiences than others, teachers must take care that the level of discrepancy is appropriate for the learners.

Six general categories of discrepancies are identified in New York State's Elementary Science Syllabus (1984). These are
• a goal to achieve without a means to achieve it
Example: I want to raise this box, but it is too heavy to lift.
• a difference between what the student expects to observe and what the student actually does observe
Example: I flip the switch, but the light does not go off.
• a missing fact or facts
Example: I put seeds in soil, but they do not grow. (Student does not know that germination requires water and warmth.)
• a difference between what students observe and what they've been told

Example: I have seen wood float in water, but you tell me that this wood will sink.
- a conflict (internal or external) between interpretations, opinions, attitudes, or values

Example: You call this nail heavy, but I call it light.

Science and mathematics need not be presented as separate subjects in the early grades. The two are closely related to each other and to problem solving. Providing children with carefully selected, significant problems helps them relate events of daily life to their mathematical representations. A good problem for young children has these characteristics:
- The problem is interesting to the child.
- The problem has mathematically demonstrable significance.
- The problem allows many different physical embodiments.
- To solve the problem, the child must modify or transform the materials used.
- The problem allows different levels of solution.
- The child believes he or she can solve the problem and knows when the solution has been reached.

Problem-solving activities can be organized around the process skills of classifying; comparing; ordering; measuring; organizing data, shape, and space; and seeing patterns.

Developmental Considerations

A child's mind differs from an adult's mind. The child's perception of physical causality changes throughout the various stages of cognitive development. That much is clear, but in what ways? What kinds of thinking is a child capable of in preschool, compared to the primary or upper elementary grades? How does the child's mind evolve toward adult thought patterns? How does teaching science through the direct manipulation of objects and events enrich mental development? How does the learner's developmental stage affect the learning of science—and how should it affect science teaching?

These are important but complex questions to which we do not have all the answers. But most elementary educators know enough to deplore the current drift away from process learning and concrete experience that is making science a class where reading science textbooks can replace "doing" science. Both the reading and the doing are necessary.

The science programs developed in the late 1960s and early 1970s with National Science Foundation funds (spurred in part by Sputnik's orbiting), such as the Elementary Science Study, Science Curriculum Instruction Study, and Science: A Process Approach, were composed almost exclusively of hands-on activities. In fact, to avoid the misuse of programs by teachers who might have preferred to have children read about science instead of "do" science, the writers of these programs initially furnished written materials for the teachers and not for the children. (This is not to attack reading in itself, of course; it is to recognize that doing is extremely important.) When later revised and modified by commercial publishers, these programs (and others purportedly based on the same approach) were clearly moving back toward giving more reading about science and fewer and fewer science activities. Thus, the programs being launched in elementary science in the 1980s by national and state research teams are clearly an attempt to reverse the tide and move towards "hands-on" science. However, many teachers resist this approach if they are given a choice. It is clearly harder to manage activity science than to have children sit at their desks and read about science. But research consistently points out that people do not learn to solve real problems as well by reading about them as by also working on them.

We also know that hands-on activities in the early years require an integration of science and mathematics methods. Children must be able to measure amounts of change to observe changes in systems. They then can begin to infer causes. Children must learn to count and measure before they can evaluate variables.

The ability to measure lets us ask and answer specific questions about relationships in systems. We need to be sure that children perceive each measurement they make as one that yields useful information. Otherwise, they see the process as pointless busywork.

Children may imitate what they see an adult doing without grasping why the action should be done in that particular way. The idea that the world is a predictable place has yet to develop in many five- to seven-year olds. Children this age have not yet developed the concept of cause-and-effect relationships and cannot see the need for consistency: They are not yet prepared to relate results to the means by which they are produced. Children are not motivated to perform measurements in physical systems if the data do not eventually yield an "Aha!"

Designing problem-solving experiences for the young learner, then, is much more than just ordering the concepts in some logical fashion and presenting them with sufficient drill and reinforcement. Learning must be active, and activities must be appropriate for particular students at particular levels of perception of physical causes. Allowances must always be made for variations in development—students of varying levels exist in every group.

Elementary School Research

J. S. Bruner, J. J. Goodnow, and G. A. Austin (1956) suggest that one of the important benefits of discovery learning can be to move the learner from such extrinsic rewards as parent or teacher approval to intrinsic motivation. Research by J. W. Atkinson (1958) and others confirms that problem-solving activity can be rewarding enough by itself to motivate learners.

Some learning theorists have expressed concern that using verbal rewards that are incongruent with behavior will result in less efficient problem-solving behavior than either a neutral, no-reward situation or praise congruent with problem-solving behavior (Lawlor, 1970). Teachers should evaluate their use of praise carefully to ensure that they are using praise accurately, not reflexively.

The ability to avoid premature closure appears to be fundamental to problem solving in science. A successful problem solver isolates possible causal variables and then tests their effects singly or in combination until a solution is found. W. Wollman, B. Eylon, and A. E. Lawson (1980) conducted an analysis of premature closure in science across developmental stages. These researchers found that subjects who could avoid premature closure initially were also capable of generating their own reasoning strategies spontaneously to solve complex inference problems. They also found that subjects who at first could not tolerate ambiguity in tasks could begin to do so after only minimal teaching. The researchers suggest that teachers who emphasize the tentativeness and probabilistic nature of all knowledge and leave some questions unanswered can help students to begin to avoid premature closure.

R. P. Theil and K. D. George (1976) examined four factors that may affect the use of one skill: prediction. They defined prediction as the acquired ability to use one or more rules from the same or different rule classes to determine the outcome of an event or series of events. The four significant factors were experience, ability to use rules, the types of rules used, and the difficulty of the task. The study concluded that elementary science curricula should focus on the basic process skills, on levels within these skills, and on the rules needed to use the process skills.

In his analysis of the problem-solving process, W. E. Muller (1983) found six properties of the learning context most closely tied to conceptualization. They are
- frequency of observation

- saliency of particular observations
- deliberation time between observations
- the order in which observations are made
- shifts in structural patterns
- transitional probabilities between observations

J. A. Shymansky, J. E. Penick, C. C. Matthews, and R. G. Good (1977) concluded that students with poor self-perception may not learn well from problem-solving science activities. Only those students who feel secure enough in their abilities to work on activities independently are in a position to benefit fully from activity-centered programs. This does not mean that easily discouraged students cannot participate in problem-solving activities (Gardner, 1985; Fuerstein, Rand, Hoffman, and Miller, 1980). Teachers and administrators must demonstrate the belief that, with proper mediation and instruction, all children can improve their abilities and their capacities for learning.

Some proponents of Piaget's theories—particularly H. G. Furth (Rosskopf, Steffe, and Taback, 1971)—hold that the traditional 3Rs curriculum for early elementary school should be abandoned in favor of a curriculum for thinking. Furth believes the knowledge content in the years before the fifth grade to be considerably less important than the opportunities provided for the child's knowing. Current practices in far too many classrooms appear to offer little provocation for thinking. Because the solution to this problem lies in the preparation of teachers, we might consider what's being done in programs for developing the thinking skills of older learners.

Toward Improvement in Problem Solving

Many people who elect elementary teaching as a profession do not consider themselves particularly strong in science and math. They are likely to be in the very large group of college students who have weak problem-solving skills. Research is needed to verify this data, and programs must be developed to provide remediation in problem solving for students of elementary education who need it. Xavier University in New Orleans has developed Project SOAR to help such students. About 175 students participate in Project SOAR each summer. Students in the program whose initial Scholastic Aptitude Tests fell below 700 have increased an average of 110 points (Hunter, Jones, Vincent, and Carmichael, 1982) after it.

We need problem-centered science curricula for both prospective teachers and young students. The design of these curricula should not be left solely to science specialists (who may not know early childhood learning theory) or solely to teachers (who may not know enough science). Programs and materials should be designed collaboratively and tested extensively.

The interdisciplinary teams that were put together in the national curriculum writing projects of the 1960s and 1970s should be a model for today's teams. The ideas from these projects also should be used to assemble a problem-centered science curriculum for the 1990s. Local needs are also important to consider in each program's design, but a national perspective is necessary to make the most of the effort invested in improving students' problem-solving skills.

Newer areas of education research also should be included. The concept of wait-time (Rowe, 1969, March; 1973; 1974a; 1974b; 1976); new paradigms for understanding the properties and functions of the brain (such as those cited by Coulter and Johnson, 1982); studies of direct and indirect teacher influence on learning (Amidon and Flanders, 1967); and research on thinking (Costa, 1984, November; Perkins, 1981) are topics of particular importance. The need for information-processing and problem-solving skills is going to be even more critical in the future than it is today. Research in problem solving, curriculum improvement, and improved programs in teacher education must be national priorities. Schools do not have the resources to meet these needs alone. National professional associations, such as the National Science Teachers Association, the Association for the Study of Cognitive Development, and the National Association for Research in Science Teaching, also must continue to work to develop our students' problem-solving and thinking skills.

References

Amidon, E., and Flanders, N. A. (Eds.). (1967). The effects of direct and indirect teacher influence on dependent-prone students learning geometry. In *Interaction analysis: Theory, research, and application.* Reading, MA: Addison-Wesley.

Atkinson, J. W. (Ed). (1958). *Motives in fantasy, action, and society.* Princeton, NJ: Van Nostrand.

Bruner, J. S., Goodnow, J. J., and Austin, G. A. (1956). *A study of thinking.* New York: John Wiley.

Costa, A. L. (1984, November). Mediating the metacognitive. *Educational Leadership, 42,* 57-62.

Coulter, D. J., and Johnson, V. R. (1982, March). Myelin and maturation: A fresh look at Piaget. *The Science Teacher, 49*(3), 43.

Fuerstein, R., Rand, Y., Hoffman, M., and Miller, R. (1980). *Instrumental enrichment: An intervention program for cognitive modifiability.* Baltimore, MD: University Park Press.

Gardner, H. (1985). *Frames of mind.* New York: Basic Books.

Hunter, J., Jones, L., Vincent, H., and Carmichael, J. W. (1982, Winter). Project SOAR: Teaching cognitive skills in precollege programs. *Journal of Learning Skills, 1,* 24-26.

Lawlor, F. X. (1970). The effects of verbal reward on the behavior of children in the primary grades at a cognitive task typical of the new elementary science curricula. *Journal of Research in Science Teaching, 7*(4), 327-340.

Muller, W. E., Jr. (1972). An analysis of the problem-solving process as a learning context and its relationship to conceptualization in elementary school science (Doctoral dissertation, Columbia University). *Dissertation Abstracts International, 33,* SECA1985 (University Microfilms No. AG72-30342).

New York State Education Department. (1984). *Elementary Science Syllabus K-6.* Albany, NY: Bureau of General Education Curriculum Development.

Perkins, D. N. (1981). *The mind's best work.* Cambridge, MA: Harvard University Press.

Rosskopf, M., Steffe, L., and Taback, S. (Eds.). (1971). *Piagetian cognitive-development research and mathemetical education: Proceedings of Conference at Columbia University* (New York [1970, October]). Reston, VA: National Council of Teachers of Mathematics.

Rowe, M. B. (1969, March). Science, silence, and sanctions. *Science and Children, 6*(6), 11-13.

Rowe, M. B. (1973). *Teaching science as continuous inquiry.* New York: McGraw-Hill.

Rowe, M. B. (1974a). Wait-time and rewards as instructional variables: Their influence on language, logic, and fate control, part I: Fate control. *Journal of Research in Science Teaching, 11*(2), 81-94.

Rowe, M. B. (1974b). Relation of wait-time and rewards to the development of language, logic, and fate control, part II: Rewards. *Journal of Research in Science Teaching, 11*(4), 291-308.

Rowe, M. B. (1976, October 15). *Using the inquiry method to teach basic skills.* Paper presented at the National Association of Biology Teachers, Denver, CO.

Shymansky, J. A., Penick, J. E., Matthews, C. C., and Good, R. G. (1977). A study of student classroom behavior and self-perception as it relates to problem solving. *Journal of Research in Science Teaching, 14*(3), 191-198.

Theil, R. P., and George, K. D. (1976). Some factors affecting the use of the science process skill of prediction by elementary children. *Journal of Research in Science Teaching, 13*(2), 155-156.

Wollman, W., Eylon, B., and Lawson, A. E. (1980). An analysis of premature closure in science and developmental stages. *Journal of Research in Science Teaching, 17*(2), 105-114.

Problem Solving in Middle Level Science

Stanley L. Helgeson
*The Ohio State University
Columbus, Ohio*

P roblem solving has been a concern of science education for at least three quarters of a century. In examining 60 years of literature as represented by articles published in *Science Education*, A. B. Champagne and L. E. Klopfer (1977) note that the first article in the first volume of the journal,* written by John Dewey, asserted that "the method of science—problem solving through reflective thinking—should be both the method and valued outcome of science instruction in America's schools" (p. 438). Today's science educators agree with Dewey and one another on the importance of problem solving in school science but are far from agreeing on the method or even the terms used to describe it. Instead of defining problem solving, we science educators have often tried to categorize and describe the process by which solutions are obtained. When we speak of scientific method, scientific thinking, critical thinking, inquiry skills, and science processes, however, we may often be talking about problem solving (Champagne and Klopfer, 1981a, January).

Approximately half the students in the United States take no science beyond the 10th grade (Helgeson, Blosser, and Howe, 1977). For these students, science in middle school or junior high may be the last course they encounter in the field. It thus becomes important to consider problem solving in the middle/junior high school context.

P. E. Blosser (1982) describes the emergence of the middle school from its forerunner, the junior high school. There is not complete agreement about why the junior high originally developed. Some claim that it was intended to increase the school's holding power, to offer both vocational and academic programs, and to provide students with the opportunity to explore a variety of subjects to help

---

*Then named *General Science Quarterly*.

them make career choices. In time, the junior high school came to be viewed as a bridge connecting elementary school to senior high school. But, while the junior high *school's* role was recognized, that of the junior high school *student* may not have been. P. D. Hurd (1978) has characterized the early adolescent as "unrecognized, underprivileged, and undereducated" (p. 55). Middle schools began to develop in the 1950s because of dissatisfaction with the program and structure of the junior high school, combined with knowledge about the following:

- changes in maturation levels
- problems of children moving from educational level to level
- new educational ideas
- developments in learning theory
- innovations in educational materials
- changes in society (Malinka, 1981, p. 3)

The importance of problem solving in middle/junior high school science is reflected in the results of S. J. Rakow's 1985 study. A group of middle/junior high school science teachers reviewed reports on the status of science education to determine criteria for excellence at that level. They concluded that an exemplary middle/junior high school science program is one that, among other things, develops students' problem-solving skills. Rakow notes that the objectives identified in this study were substantially the same as those identified by the NSTA Task Force on Excellence in Middle/Junior High School Science Programs (Reynolds, Pitotti, Rakow, Thompson, and Wohl, 1984).

Assessing Problem Solving

The literature about science education reflects the close relationship between problem-solving and science process skills. In most cases problem solving is, in effect, defined by the skills that are measured or assessed; such definitions usually include the processes of science. In an overview of measurement instruments in science, V. J. Mayer and J. M. Richmond (1982) note the increased attention paid to science process skills and problem-solving behavior during the curriculum development activities of the 1960s. However, the development of instruments to measure or assess these skills and behaviors clearly did not keep pace; Mayer and Richmond include in their overview only two instruments aimed at the junior high/middle school level. Most of the instruments available today have been developed since the 1960s.

One of those early instruments for evaluating problem solving was discussed by D. P. Butts (1964), H. L. Jones (1966), and Butts and Jones (1966). Originally called the X-35 Test of Problem Solving, it became known as the TAB[*] Inventory of Science Processes and later as the TAB Science Test. In this test, by whatever name, the student is presented with a situation involving a physics-focus film based on the Suchman discrepant event format[†] and is asked to select an explanation from a given list. The student is then faced with clue questions whose answers are covered by the tabs that give the TAB test its name. The student removes the tab from each question and places the tab on an answer sheet. Under each tab is a yes or no indicating whether the explanation is correct. The student continues until he or she finds a correct explanation. By looking at the tabs in the order in which they were removed, the investigator can determine what questions were asked and in what order.

---

[*]See box 1 for a list of acronyms and abbreviations of curriculums and measuring instruments.

[†]For example, one Suchman discrepant event film depicts a beaker of coffee placed under a bell jar and apparently boiling at room temperature. See page 27.

The TAB Science Puzzler, derived from the TAB Science Test and designed by R. E. Norton (1971), has five subtasks that coincide with the steps of a generally accepted problem-solving model:
1. Problem Orientation
2. Problem Identification
3. Problem Solution
4. Data Analysis
5. Problem Verification

Box 1: Acronyms

ES—Environmental Studies

ESCP—Earth Science Curriculum Project

GALT—Group Assessment of Logical Thinking

IMB—Interaction of Man* and the Biosphere

IPS—Introductory Physical Science curriculum

IQ—Intelligence Quotient

ORES—Objective Referenced Evaluation in Science

SAPA—Science—A Process Approach
> originally developed in the late 1950s and early 1960s by
> the American Association for the Advancement of Science

SAPA II—Science—A Process Approach
> a second generation version of SAPA

SRA—Stanford Research Associates

TAB—Not really an acronym, the TAB test is so named
> because of the tabs that cover answers to its questions

TIPS—Test of Integrated Process Skills

TIPS II—Test of Integrated Process Skills, second version

TOLT—Test of Logical Thinking

TOPSS—Test of Problem-Solving Skills

TSM—Time, Space, and Matter curriculum

USMES—Unified Science and Mathematics for Elementary School

*That is, humans.

Another group of instruments shares several characteristics. All are multiple-choice tests designed to measure science process skills, such as identifying and controlling variables, interpreting data, formulating hypotheses, defining operationally (i.e., defining a variable by its actions or effects), and graphing and interpreting data.* These instruments were developed by R. S. Tannenbaum (1969); D. W. Fyffe (1972); R. W. Robison (1974); J. A. Ross and F. J. Maynes (1983a, 1983b); and L. Cronin and M. J. Padilla (1986, March).

Box 2: Science Process Skills

identifying variables

controlling variables

defining operationally

formulating hypotheses

graphing data

interpreting data

---

*See box 2 for a list of science process skills.

Two closely related tests are the Test of Integrated Process Skills (TIPS) designed by F. J. Dillashaw and J. R. Okey (1980) and a second version, TIPS II, developed by J. C. Burns, Okey, and K. C. Wise (1985). Both are 36-item multiple-choice tests for middle and secondary school students covering content from all science areas. The items, which offer four possible answers from which students choose, are related to five integrated process skills.

K. G. Tobin and W. Capie (1981) constructed the Test of Logical Thinking (TOLT), a 10-item test for students of middle school age and older. The instrument contains five pairs of items, each set related to one of five modes of logical thought—to identifying and controlling variables and to four ways of reasoning: proportional, correlational, probabilistic, and combinatorial. Based on the internal consistency of the test and on students' performances on problems in interviews and on tests of integrated science skills, Tobin and Capie concluded that the TOLT provides a means of measuring formal reasoning.

Two instruments were developed as part of projects to evaluate science curriculum materials. T. J. Shaw (1982) developed a test of process skills using a multiple-choice format as part of a study to examine the effects on problem-solving skills of a process-oriented curriculum, Science—A Process Approach II (SAPA II)—the second generation of the 1950s and 1960s SAPA curriculums. The process skills Shaw measured were the same as those Tobin and Capie investigated. M. H. Shann (1976) developed the Test of Problem-Solving Skills (TOPSS) as part of the evaluation of the Unified Science and Mathematics for Elementary School (USMES). Again, the test was a multiple-choice instrument designed to measure the following process steps:
- define problems
- suggest hypotheses
- select procedures
- draw conclusions
- evaluate critically
- reason quantitatively

Research reveals considerable agreement that problem solving calls for the science process skills and *can* be measured; there are instruments available with sufficient validity and reliability. It is also clear that, if problem solving is to be an important outcome of science instruction, it must be among the outcomes we measure. There is no use listing problem solving as an objective of instruction without including it in the evaluation of instruction.

Problem-Solving Strategies and Behaviors

Several studies deal with the strategies students exhibit as they engage in problem-solving behavior. J. T. Wilson (1973, March) investigated the effect of generated hunches upon subsequent search activities in problem-solving situations. His students, divided into three groups, observed a contradictory stimulus. Wilson asked the first group to write hunches, the second group to read hunches, and the third group neither to read nor to write hunches. His findings suggest that arranging learning conditions so that hunches are generated can positively influence search activities and the quality of the solutions generated. In effect, the students became more efficient problem solvers.

Two related studies by M. E. Quinn and K. D. George (1975) and Quinn and C. Kessler (1980, April) examined hypothesis formation by sixth-grade students. The studies found that
- Hypothesis formation can be taught.
- Given instruction, children from lower socioeconomic groups hypothesized as well as ones from upper levels.

• The ability to hypothesize is correlated positively with intelligence, overall grade-point average, and reading ability.
• Bilingual children performed better than did monolingual children.
Because children educated in more than one language appear to be better problem solvers than their monolingual peers, the authors recommend closer working relationships between science and language teachers.

E. G. Schmiess (1970/1971) attempted to determine whether sixth-grade students could engage successfully in scientific investigation. Schmiess measured the students' success by their proficiency in solving problems, interest in science, and ability to solve new problems. Schmiess found that
• Fifty percent of the class was accurate on 78 percent of their investigations.
• Posttest scores on science interest and on solving new problems were significantly higher than pretest scores.
• High and average achievers were significantly higher than low achievers on ability to solve new problems.
• No significant differences in interest in science were obtained among high, average, and low achievers.
• No significant differences were found between boys and girls in solving selected science problems, interest in science, or ability to solve new problems.

A. Mandell (1980) conducted a study to identify common problem-solving behaviors and strategies used by the 10 sixth graders whom teachers had classified out of 25 students as superior problem solvers. A secondary purpose was to determine whether the classification had been accurate. The students classified as successful problem solvers had significantly higher means on IQ tests and on Stanford Research Associates (SRA) Math and Science subtests than the other 15. In an individual, tape-recorded interview, each student was encouraged to think aloud about a series of six problems presented in the same order. All 10 of the students selected by two or three teachers as superior problem solvers were successful. Mandell found that the students in the successful group had five common characteristics:

1. They were quick to identify the nature of the problem.
2. They were able to use all four abilities in Piaget's categories—identification, negation, reciprocity, and correlativity.
3. They were not dependent on physical manipulations or calculations to solve most problems.
4. They used rough tables or matrices if calculations were needed.
5. They expressed their reasoning and procedures with ease.

C. F. Berger (1982) and Berger and P. R. Pintrich (1986) reported studies examining how well students learned to use science processes. A computer simulation presented a vertical line or "wall" on the right side of the screen, with a circle representing a balloon touching the wall at a predetermined vertical distance. Students were to estimate the height of the balloon; as they entered their estimations into the computer, an arrow appeared on the left side of the screen, traveled to the right, and stuck in the wall at the height of the estimate. The students identified three basic patterns of movement: random, "ladder" (moving up or down systematically), or "bracket" (moving in a high-low sequence and gradually closing in on target). The researchers found, among other things, that the microcomputer provided a useful and powerful tool to gather strategy data, that students used effective strategies and improved their estimation skill quickly, and that age and amount of information presented in the task affected performance. Younger students did not perform as well as older students, a finding consistent with other studies of developmental differences in learning and memory. As the amount of information available increased, students showed a decrease in reaction time, indicating less demand on short-term memory. With this decrease, performance improved.

Champagne and Klopfer (1981b) investigated the interaction between semantic knowledge and process skills in eighth-grade students' performance in solving two types of problems—analogies and set membership. Champagne and Klopfer concluded that, as they had hypothesized, successful performance on analogy problems designed to determine a structure for the science concepts presented cannot be attributed to differences in the students' processing skills. For set membership problems, however, although their edge disappeared in a comparison made one year later, students rated high in processing skills performed better at problem solving both before and after instruction.

R. R. Ronning and D. W. McCurdy (1982) reported a study that included examining the problem-solving processes of 150 junior high school students as well as a training program in problem-solving processes designed for that age group. Each student was given a set of six problems selected to resemble the problems in junior high school science textbooks. No significant grade-level differences were found for students in the seventh, eighth, and ninth grades, although a trend to higher scores at higher grade levels was evident. While boys' performances at all grade levels exceeded that of girls slightly, the gender factor was insignificant. The junior high school students studied had a generally positive attitude toward science as interesting and necessary. At the same time, paradoxically, they regarded science as difficult, unimaginative, hard to understand, and requiring much memorization (p. 35). The junior high school students in Ronning and McCurdy's study "evinced not even rudimentary general problem attack skills" (p. 31). Ronning and McCurdy note that many junior high curriculums include the four- or five-step "scientific method" in an effort to provide students with a strategy for attacking problems. However, the evidence from the attempt to teach such a general process suggests that seventh graders are perhaps developmentally unable to profit from it (p. 38). The evidence further suggests that a hands-on approach to teaching science, using tasks to pique curiosity, may help students approach problems more skillfully and solve them more successfully. According to Ronning and McCurdy, teachers should "introduce and regularly reinforce problem attack skills such as looking for constants and variables, generating and testing hypotheses, etc." (p. 38).

A. N. Rudnitsky and C. R. Hunt (1986) conducted a study to examine and describe strategies used by children to solve a complex problem inviting them to discover a set of cause and effect relationships. The students, from grades four through six, were told that a dot of light on the computer represented a vehicle which could be moved by colored keys on the keyboard. The problem was to determine what effect each colored key had on the vehicle. The students had to make two or three keystrokes at a time to make the vehicle move; the program would not accept fewer than two or more than three keystrokes. The researchers identified four different types of move sequences:

• *Explorations* occurred when the subjects were trying combinations of moves freely, often ignoring the restrictions on the number of keystrokes.

• *Patterns* repeated a particular two or three keystroke sequence.

• *Focusing* involved applying a strategy, such as putting together various combinations of keystrokes or pursuing a hunch about the effect of a particular key. This systematic process often generated information that could be transformed into a theory or testable hypothesis.

• *Hypothesis testing* involved making and trying out a prediction. Not all hypotheses were correct and testable; not all led to correct answers. Typically, however, one or two successful predictions generated enough evidence for students to draw conclusions.

This study supports the position that theories do not exist in nature, waiting to be plucked; rather, they must be constructed. Thus, if we are to help students develop skill in problem solving, we must provide activities that ask them to generate theories.

Research indicates that there has been at least some success in identifying students who are successful problem solvers and who can identify the nature of problems, manipulate and interpret data, and reason abstractly. Furthermore, some aspects of problem-solving skills *can* be taught, and practice in these skills is beneficial. However, we must bear in mind that at least some part of problem-solving ability is probably related to the students' level of cognitive development. Among other studies, the work of Ronning and McCurdy (discussed above) and of A. E. Lawson and W. T. Wollman (below) suggests that attempting to teach a general problem-solving method to students between 10 and 13 years old is likely to fail. If we are to succeed, we must include multiple approaches in our teaching to provide for individual differences among our students, and we must deal with problem solving in specific cases, permitting students to apply learned strategies to problems that are new but not totally unfamiliar.

Cognitive Style and Problem Solving

Five investigations dealt with students' cognitive styles or preferences in relationship to problem solving. Ronning, McCurdy, and R. Ballinger (1984) examined the relationship of problem-solving success to field independence or field dependence* of junior high school students. The researchers found that
• Junior high school students have difficulty with problem solving, especially when problems involve proportional reasoning or separation and control of variables.
• Field-independent students significantly out-performed field-dependent students on solving the problems.
• No gender differences were found for problem solving.

Lawson and Wollman (1977) conducted a study that examined, among other things, the relationship between sixth graders' performance on Piagetian tasks (bending rods and balancing beams) and their field dependence or independence. In this study, as in others, a significant correlation was found between success on these particular tasks and degree of field independence. The authors' findings imply that, if we wish to enhance problem-solving success, we can foster autonomy by allowing students to investigate phenomena freely. Inquiry and discovery methods that encourage autonomy and initiative may foster field independence and, therefore, cognitive development. Science classrooms should provide a variety of increasingly complex and repeated experiences. It appears likely that such experiences will occur most readily when students investigate real science phenomena with direct, hands-on activities.

In a five-year study published in 1973, N. C. Scott, Jr., examined the longitudinal effects of the inquiry strategy method on students' styles of categorization. The experimental students received two to three years of inquiry strategy in their late elementary or junior high school science classes, while the comparison students were exposed to conventional science teaching during their elementary, junior, and senior high school years. The longitudinal study tested both groups twice, once at the end of seventh grade and again before graduation from high school. The tests indicated that the inquiry process had a persistent, positive effect on the experimental students' analytical behavior: They maintained a significant advantage over the comparison students for six years.

---

*This concept is used here as in M. U. Smith's paper in this volume. Smith summarizes: "Consider field dependence as measured by the Group Embedded Figures Test (Witkin, Oltman, Raskin, and Karp, 1971). Individuals who can 'break up an organized visual field in order to keep part of it separate from that field' are field independent (p. 4); individuals who do not have this ability are field dependent."

K. G. Jacknicke and D. A. Pearson (1979, March) investigated the influence of the reflective versus impulsive dimension on students' problem-solving skills in elementary school science. The sixth graders involved were classified in disposition as reflective, as impulsive, or as neither reflective nor impulsive. The problem-solving tasks required either a guided-discovery approach or an open-ended approach for completion. Analysis showed that

- "Reflectives" and "impulsives" performed about equally well in selecting and generating observations and hypotheses and in evaluating these observations and hypotheses.
- "Reflectives" and "impulsives" asked similar types and quantities of questions during the problem-solving process.
- The "reflectives" did better than the "impulsives" in selecting and generating hypotheses appropriate to the different content and modes of presentation in guided-discovery and open-ended tasks.
- Observing and hypothesizing abilities appear in this study to be more task-specific than R. M. Gagne (1965) suggests; that is, the abilities do not transfer easily to different kinds of problems.

D. L. Dunlop and F. Fazio (1975, March) studied the relationship between abstract preferences in problem-solving tasks and the ability to abstract and think formally. Abstraction scores were determined by having students indicate their preference for which methods they chose to solve specified problems. An assumption underlying Dunlop and Fazio's study was that the level of abstract reasoning students use to solve problems is often substantially below their actual capacity. As expected, older groups, with a greater percentage of students in the formal operational stage of development, demonstrated greater abstract-reasoning ability. However, no significant differences emerged among grade levels with respect to abstract preference scores. This preference was found to be independent of ability to abstract and the development of formal operational thought. The results supported the conclusion that a preference for a concrete algorithm in a problem-solving situation was not dependent upon an ability to abstract. The assumption that students often reason at a level below their capacities is supported by this study.

Several of these findings are important to us as science teachers. First, as most middle/junior high school teachers realize, their students find problem solving difficult. This is particularly true when the problems involve the separation and control of variables. Next, students frequently do not operate at capacity in solving problems; their preference for a particular method or approach to a solution may limit their success. Third, it is clear from the research that field-independent students are more successful in solving problems than are field-dependent students. Because it appears that problem solving is not easily generalized, it is in the best interest of our students to provide a variety of kinds of problems in our science programs. Fourth, inquiry experience throughout the middle school years may result in an advantage that will persist for some years in the future.

Cognitive Development and Reasoning Ability

Several studies examined the relationship of various aspects of reasoning ability to cognitive development. As can be seen, reasoning is usually considered to include such skills as identifying and controlling variables, interpreting data, and hypothesizing—skills that are also related to problem solving.

M. C. Linn and D. I. Levine (1976) conducted a developmental investigation of students' ability to control variables. They found that

- There were no consistent gender differences in performance across problems for any questions.
- Familiarity with the variable and format of the questions influenced success.

• There was a qualitative change in the ability to control variables between the ages of 12 and 16.

The investigators concluded that there was some evidence to support the hypothesis that subjects frequently try to solve new problems by drawing upon apparently relevant past experience.

A study by J. R. Staver (1986) investigated the effects of task format and number of independent variables on the responses of eighth-grade students to a reasoning problem involving control of variables. There were two levels of numbers of independent variables (two to three and four to five) and two task formats for response (essay and multiple choice). The study showed that

• Task format had no effect on the subjects' scores.

• The number of independent variables resulted in significant differences in mean scores for the essays; for the multiple-choice format, however, there was a rather uniform distribution of mean scores.

• The two-to-three variable versions were significantly less difficult than the four-to-five ones.

The knowledge and procedures the students used to solve these problems are contained in working memory. Staver's results indicate that a task adding independent variables to controlled ones can overload working memory, thus affecting performance. Science teachers must pay close attention to the demands made on working memory both during instruction and evaluation.

A study by W. L. Saunders and J. Jesunathadas (1988) found that ninth graders performed better on proportional reasoning problems involving familiar content than on those involving unfamiliar content. A major concern was whether students' problem-solving abilities generalize across subject matter domains. The researchers found that content familiarity interacted with difficulty; that is, this difference in performance was more pronounced on work with easy problems than on that with difficult ones.

Padilla, Okey, and Dillashaw (1983) examined the relationship between integrated process skills and the formal thinking abilities of middle and high school students. The researchers used the TIPS to measure the five integrated skills. Formal thinking ability was measured by Tobin and Capie's TOLT.* The evidence shows that science process skill is strongly associated with logical thinking. Further research is needed to determine whether a process skill improves or discourages logical thinking ability and to find out whether teaching for one kind of ability will affect the other.

C. R. Coble reported a comparison study involving middle grade students in North Carolina and Japan (1986, March), W. E. Spooner (1986, March), and F. E. Mattheis, Coble, and Spooner (1986, March). The primary purpose of the study was to measure reasoning skills,† integrated process skills, and their relationship to each other, of students in grades seven, eight, and nine in the two countries. North Carolina students had a more positive attitude toward science than did their Japanese counterparts at all grade levels, but the North Carolina students' attitude scores decreased from the seventh to the ninth grade. Male and female students from both places scored about the same in integrated process skills (TIPS II), which increased progressively from the seventh to the ninth grade. The most difficult area for the Americans was identifying variables. In

---

*See above in this paper, page 16.

†Reasoning skills were measured by the Group Assessment of Logical Thinking (GALT), a test closely related to the TOLT.

contrast, the Japanese scored highest on this subscale; their mean score was also significantly higher than that of the North Carolina students.

A significant relationship, which is consistent with findings in other similar studies, emerged between scores on integrated process skills and on logical thinking (TOLT). The results on the logical thinking test indicated that only 10 percent of the North Carolina students were functioning at the formal operational stage. In comparison, 32 percent of the Japanese students were functioning in the formal mode. Thus, cultural factors appear to be at least as significant as developmental factors.

Two reports summarized research on reasoning ability, particularly that ability, implied by formal thought, to apply general principles of problem solving to specific problems. Linn and Levine (1977) reviewed the research on scientific reasoning and found that while changes in this area did take place during adolescence, they were not as complete as suggested by earlier descriptions of formal thought. Linn and Levine found that performance, as related to scientific reasoning, appeared to be influenced by

• the number of variables to be considered
• the student's familiarity and previous experience with variables
• the method of presenting information about the task
• the procedure for interacting with the apparatus (e.g., free or constrained)
• the subject matter of the problem (physics, biology, etc.)

Linn and Levine reached five conclusions of importance for instruction. First, only a small number of the adolescents studied could effectively control variables in familiar situations. Second, relatively few adolescents had reached the level of formal operations; therefore, concrete experience is a valuable aid to learning at all stages of adolescence. Third, programs that offer a choice of mode of learning or that provide several approaches for teaching a principle are more useful than programs that adhere to a single theory. Fourth, programs that encourage learners to manipulate materials could have great benefit. Finally, the method that learners use to organize information is important: It should emphasize strategies for solution that promote organization.

Staver (1984) examined research on formal reasoning patterns in science education in terms of implications for science teachers. The research evidence suggests five conclusions:

First, adolescents and young adults quite frequently do not use formal reasoning patterns even when such thinking is necessary to comprehend fully a segment of learning.

Second, different students may perform the same tasks in a different order; an adolescent may apply control-of-variables reasoning on one task before turning to another; a second student may do the tasks in reverse order.

Third, achievement in science includes both conceptual knowledge and reasoning skills.

Fourth, the conclusion that children are unable to comprehend certain concepts until they reach a certain state in their reasoning development overlooks the idea (called *constructivism*) that knowledge may be acquired by

formation within the brain, through interactions with the environment, as opposed to the *empiricist* view that the knowledge is internalized from the outside environment. The distinction between these views can be clarified by an analogy in physical development. Living systems develop by differentiation and coordination through an internal genetic code and interaction with the environment (a *constructivist* model), rather than by addition of nutrients from the outside environment. . . .

Physical knowledge (size, shape, color of an object) is present in the environment and can be acquired through observation. Suppose, however, a child is given a red ball and a blue ball. Whereas the red and blue balls are observable, their difference is not. The difference is a relationship, mentally constructed from within by the mind. (pp. 578–579, italics added)

Concepts of the first kind can be successfully taught by direct transmission (telling). Concepts involving relationships, however, require instructional activities that facilitate construction from within and that include concrete models, materials, inquiry, and discussion during the learning process.

Fifth, science teachers should design and carry out instruction that does not overtax working memory. They should create situations that involve cognitive conflicts in which difficulty is controlled and success is virtually assured at frequent points.

The evidence strongly associates science process skills with logical thinking. It also suggests that both cognitive development and problem-solving skills are related to maturation. The ability to control variables tends to increase (within limits) with age; however, control of variables may vary from student to student and from one task to another by the same student. Adolescents frequently do not operate at the formal operations level. If we are to maximize opportunities for both cognitive development and problem solving, we need to limit the number of variables involved in problems, to draw upon familiar examples when possible, and to allow freedom of interaction with equipment and materials in direct, concrete, hands-on experience.

Problem Solving and Instruction

A large segment of the science education research dealing with problem solving is related to the effects of various aspects of instruction on students' problem-solving ability.

Three studies examined the effects of classroom structure on student outcomes. J. Bowyer, B. Chen, and H. D. Thier (1976) studied the effects of a free-choice environment on sixth graders' ability to control variables. Half of the students were randomly assigned to a group with access to a science enrichment center where they could freely select science activities and materials. Among other findings, the researchers noted that more than 60 percent of the students within all subgroups did not control variables at all, around 32 percent controlled them inconsistently, and an insignificant number controlled them appropriately. As a result of the program, however, approximately one-third of the experimental population changed from being unaware of the need to control variables to recognizing that experiments need controls. After instruction, 78 percent of the experimental group understood the necessity for controlling variables, particularly familiar ones such as weight and length.

D. J. McKee (1978, March) investigated the effects on sixth graders in science classes of two contrasting teachers' behaviors. McKee studied the students' science achievement, problem-solving ability, confidence, and classroom demeanor in response, on the one hand, to a student-structured learning pattern, which minimized restrictions, and, on the other, a teacher-structured learning pattern, which was moderately restrictive. One hundred students in four classes worked for 15 weeks, at the end of which each student was interviewed individually to assess problem-solving ability and confidence. McKee concluded that, because the student-structured strategy worked better to improve problem-solving skills, this strategy was the obvious choice for teachers interested in promoting students' ability to solve problems while improving self-confidence.

G. W. Foster (1982, April) set out to determine whether cooperative small groups would stimulate the creativity of fifth- and sixth-grade students more than an individualized learning environment. Half of the students worked alone, while the other half worked together in groups of four or five. Each half worked in a student-structured environment on the same science activity, which involved creating as many different types of electrical circuits as possible from a given set of batteries and bulbs. The same trained teacher guided students in both the individual and small-group settings. Among other things, Foster found that both fifth and sixth graders did significantly better at creating electrical circuits in small groups than they did working alone.

The findings reported by Foster are supported in the research on cooperative learning summarized by R. T. Johnson and D. W. Johnson (1989). They note the need for social cooperation as an active part of learning and, based upon research, cite four advantages of such learning methods:

> • Cooperative learning experiences promote more learning and more retention than competitive or individualistic learning experiences. . . .
> • The more difficult the material, the wider the gap in achievement favoring cooperative over competitive or individualistic learning. . . .
> • Cooperative learning experiences tend to create higher levels of self-esteem and healthier processes for achieving a sense of self-worth than do competitive or individualistic learning experiences. . . .
> • Acceptance of differences, which comes with successful cooperative experiences, is important to gifted science students*. . . . (pp. 322–323)

Another series of four studies examined types of instruction and problem solving. K. L. Egolf (1979) examined the effects of two modes of instruction on seventh- and eighth-grade students' abilities to solve quantitative word problems in science. Researcher-developed booklets were used to teach the students how to solve a specific quantitative word problem related to density and to teach a general method for solving word problems. Among the conclusions drawn were that the booklets could be used effectively to teach students how to solve density problems; that no booklet successfully taught the students a general problem-solving method; that significant grade-level effects existed regarding ability to solve word problems; and that gender was unrelated to the problem-solving ability being measured.

E. T. Brooks (1982) compared the effectiveness of mastery instruction and an equivalent nonmastery mode of instruction for improving students' learning and retention of selected science process skills. The process skills included the lower levels of observation, classification, and prediction, and the higher level skills of data analysis and hypothesizing. No significant differences were found in levels of achievement between students instructed by either method. Mastery instruction did not result in greater achievement, but, while students instructed through mastery techniques didn't necessarily learn more, they retained better what they did learn.

G. E. Glasson (1989) conducted a study comparing the relative effects of two laboratory procedures—hands-on and teacher-demonstration—on ninth graders' knowledge of two kinds—declarative (factual and conceptual) and procedural (problem solving). Glasson particularly wanted to determine, first, whether these relationships varied as a function of reasoning ability (measured by TOLT) and, next, whether reasoning ability along with prior knowledge predicted student achievement. He found that

• The two instructional methods resulted in equal amounts of declarative knowledge.
• Students in the hands-on laboratory class performed significantly better, regardless of reasoning ability, on the procedural-knowledge test than did students in the teacher-demonstration class.
• Prior knowledge significantly predicted performance on the declarative-knowledge test.

---

*While Johnson and Johnson were writing in this case specifically about students with gifts in science, acceptance of differences is, of course, essential for all students.

• Both reasoning ability and prior knowledge significantly predicted performance on the procedural-knowledge test, with reasoning ability being the stronger predictor.

J. D. Novak, G. B. Gowin, and G. T. Johansen (1983) and Novak (1989) explored the use of concept mapping and knowledge Vee mapping with seventh- and eighth-grade science students. They found that in general, students of any ability could be successful in concept mapping and that other factors (e.g., motivation) were more important than ability. Both seventh and eighth graders could acquire an understanding of the Vee-mapping technique and apply it in regular junior high school science. The experimental classes demonstrated superiority in problem-solving performance on new problems after less than six months of instruction with these strategies. The data suggested that concept mapping and Vee mapping contributed to changes in student knowledge, problem-solving skills, and performance on unfamiliar problem-solving tests. But the studies also indicated that effective use of the Vee-mapping strategy takes time for students to achieve and that two or more years may be required for students to achieve high competence.

D. A. H. Cox (1980/1981) studied seventh and eighth graders' use of selected problem-solving skills with microcomputers. The students were randomly assigned to work either alone or in groups of two, three, or five for three 50-minute sessions. Among Cox's conclusions were the following:
• Students can improve in problem-solving skills by working for a short period of time on a microcomputer.
• The training program on organizing data in a matrix was successful.
• Individuals worked better in teams than alone.
• Group interaction enabled subjects of all abilities to participate and solve problems successfully.
• All subjects adapted quickly and easily to the use of microcomputers.
• The microcomputer is a viable, motivating aid for the development of some problem-solving skills of early adolescents.

Inquiry and Problem Solving

Six studies dealt with inquiry and problem-solving strategies of instruction. Butts and Jones studied the effectiveness of inquiry training in producing more effective problem-solving behavior in sixth-grade students. The investigators concluded that students could benefit from directed instruction in problem-solving behaviors and that age, IQ, gender, and science factual knowledge were not significant factors in whether inquiry training was successful or not.

A study was conducted by M. Davis (1979) to examine the effects on achievement of upper elementary school students of two approaches to science instruction: first, through an expository text, and, next, through guided inquiry and discovery. Davis found that, in promoting knowledge of science content, the approach through guided-inquiry discovery was significantly more effective than that through the expository text. While students' understanding of science inquiry and processes was only slightly better among members of the group using guided inquiry, the latter expressed significantly more positive attitudes about science than did those working with the expository text.

Using different patterns and amounts of instruction on planning experiments with sixth- and eighth-grade students, Padilla, Okey, and K. Garrard (1984) examined the effects of instruction on integrated science process skill achievement. The results showed that students from both age groups can learn to use certain integrated process skills, that students showed the most growth in identifying variables and stating hypotheses, and that the greatest benefit seemed to result from integrating science content and process instruction over a long period of time. Differences generally favored instruction that emphasized designing and carrying out experiments. None of the treatments significantly affected formal operational ability.

Ross and Maynes (1983b) taught sixth-grade students an instructional program based on expert-novice differences in experimental problem-solving performance. The instructional design, based on a chronological account of what successful scientists do in designing experiments, emphasized two skills: developing a focus for the investigation (hypothesis formulation) and establishing a framework for the investigation (including control of variables). The instructional treatment included identifying causes and effects in experimental questions, rewriting inadequate questions, manipulating equipment, and teaching operations from the identified hierarchy of cognitive behaviors, such as identifying potential effects, measuring the results, etc. Performance was measured by tests of specific transfer; that is, students used the same skills in different experimental settings using different equipment. Because it was found that the experimental group of students consistently outperformed the controls, the investigators concluded that their program had a beneficial effect.

P. Lawsiripaiboon (1983) examined the effects of a problem-solving strategy on ninth-grade students' ability to apply and analyze physical science subject matter. The experimental group did problem-solving laboratory activities and held classroom discussions emphasizing the application and analysis levels described in Bloom's Taxonomy. The conventional group did laboratory activities and held discussions focusing on levels of knowledge and comprehension. Teachers of the problem-solving group, which significantly outperformed the conventional group, asked significantly more high-level questions. Lawsiripaiboon concluded that the problem-solving strategy used in the study seemed to be an effective means for improving overall achievement, particularly achievement at the application and analysis levels.

A similar study was reported by J. M. Russell (1979), Russell and E. L. Chiappetta (1980, April; 1981), and Chiappetta and Russell (1982). The study's purpose was to improve eighth graders' ability to apply and to analyze Earth science subject matter. Instruction for students in the experimental groups included reading, problem-solving tasks, discussion, and laboratory exercises emphasizing application and analysis. Students in the control groups received instruction from a traditional textbook and reading, discussion, and laboratory activities. Teachers of the experimental groups asked their students a higher level of questions than those posed to the controls. When the experimental groups significantly outperformed the control groups, the investigators concluded that an instructional program using a problem-solving approach will significantly increase overall achievement, particularly at the application and knowledge levels. Further, they decided that such an approach should include written problem-solving activities and teacher-directed questions that emphasize application of knowledge.

Linn, C. Clement, S. Pulos, and P. Sullivan (1989) assessed the role of instruction in science topics combined with that of logical reasoning in teaching adolescents about blood pressure. Four major findings emerged:
• All participants acquired knowledge of science topics relevant to blood pressure.
• Those receiving instruction in strategies learned about the strategy of controlling variables.
• Gaining knowledge about science topics influenced reasoning performance.
• Combining knowledge about science topics with instruction in strategies produced more generalized reasoning performance than did teaching knowledge about science topics alone.
These results show that both knowledge about science topics and instruction in strategies help students succeed by bringing relevant information to bear on solving problems.

The Suchman Inquiry Development Program was involved in three studies. W. W. Jones (1972/1983) investigated what effect acknowledging successful autonomous discovery had on seventh-grade students' problem-solving abilities, concept development, science achievement, and self-concepts as learners. Students were exposed to the Inquiry Development Program for a semester. Similar materials and techniques were used with both experimental and control classes, but, in the experimental classes, successful autonomous discovery was acknowledged by such comments as "Right," or "OK," or "That agrees with what most scientists believe at this time." Jones concluded that this acknowledgment or lack thereof did not significantly affect the seventh graders' self-concepts as learners in relation to motivation, task orientation, problem solving, or class membership; however, surprisingly, *not* acknowledging successful autonomous discovery resulted in greater science achievement gains than acknowledging it. While *neither* technique resulted in a significant change in development of science *concepts*, exposure to *either* appeared to significantly increase the problem-solving abilities of the students. This fact suggests that the discovery activity, rather than the teacher's response, was the important factor.

C. A. Pouler (1976) and Pouler and E. Wright (1977, March) investigated the effects of intensive instruction on the ability of ninth-grade students to generate written hypotheses and ask questions about variables pertaining to discrepant scientific events. During the experimental instruction, students watched a discrepant event (a Suchman film loop)* until they generated six acceptable hypotheses. The investigator then evaluated the hypotheses according to standards that reflected the type of reinforcement and instruction the student was to receive. For example, one student might be told that the hypothesis was excellent and then, for reinforcement, be given the criteria for an acceptable hypothesis, while another might be offered only the criteria. After instruction, students were shown two different discrepant events and asked to write hypotheses for one and questions for the other. Reinforcement alone increased the quantity of written hypotheses. Reinforcement plus knowledge of the criteria produced higher quality hypotheses.

In a related study, Wright (1978) examined the feasibility of intensive instruction in either the observation of details or the generation of hypotheses. He used a discrepant-event film loop similar to those mentioned above as a model for improving the open exploration skills of ninth graders. Wright concluded that soliciting hypotheses and detailed observations were equally effective instructional approaches in increasing exploration skills with one exception: The students who had been instructed in observing details observed more of them.

The research shows that students benefit from instruction in problem solving. Students can and do learn to use integrated process skills. Not only do they show improved problem-solving performance, but also they can transfer the skills learned to help with new (if not too dissimilar) problems. In addition, students who receive such instruction tend to learn more science and to have more positive attitudes toward it. The most effective approach to teaching science appears to integrate content and process skills over time, using hands-on inquiry activities.

Science Curriculums and Problem Solving

Tracing the historical development of problem solving as a curriculum goal, E. P. White (1978) notes that it has been a major strand in U. S. education from the Dewey School of 1896 onward. As this book indicates, concern with problem solving among science curriculum developers persists today.

---

*See note to page 14.

Junior high school science curriculums developed in the 1960s increased the emphasis on developing problem-solving ability rather than acquiring factual knowledge. F. E. Friot (1971) studied the relationship between inquiry teaching, as represented by these curriculums, and the development of interpropositional logic needed in problem solving. The performance of eighth and ninth graders enrolled in experimental science curriculums was evaluated at the beginning and end of the school year and compared to that of students in a control group taking general science. The study showed that logical thinking processes could be evaluated using the Piagetian tasks and that some curriculums were effective at some grade levels but not at others. The *Time, Space, and Matter* (TSM) curriculum was significantly more effective in enhancing the development of formal operations than were either the *Introductory Physical Science* (IPS) or the *Earth Science Curriculum Project* (ESCP) curriculum. At the ninth-grade level, both the ESCP and IPS curriculums were significantly better in this area than the control and the IPS curriculum was significantly better than the ESCP curriculum. Neither gender nor IQ was significantly related to gain in logical thinking ability.

G. C. Schlenker (1971) reported an investigation to determine whether the content in a physical science program for grades five through eight, taught through methods promoting development of inquiry, achieved significantly different results than a program taught traditionally. He concluded that children who studied under the inquiry-development program gained a significantly greater understanding of science and scientists and became more fluent and productive in using the skills of inquiry and their close relative, critical thinking, than did children who studied under the traditional program; however, Schlenker found no consistently significant difference between the two groups in the mastery or retention of the usual content of elementary school science.

A 1971 study by D. J. Gudaitis compared selected aspects of two seventh-grade science programs, the *Interaction of Man* * and the Biosphere* (IMB), an experimental inquiry program, and *Science is Explaining*, the control program. From pretest to posttest, students in the experimental program showed no significant change in attitude toward science, while the attitude scores of students in the control group decreased; however, there was no significant difference between the two groups in gain scores. Students in both programs showed significant growth in critical-thinking skills, but students in the experimental group made significantly greater gains in this area than did those in the control.

During the 1973–1974 school year, Shann, N. C. Reali, H. Bender, T. Aiello, and L. Hench (1975) evaluated the problem-solving abilities of students randomly selected from each of 38 classes which were using the USMES program. (See above page 16.) The students, working in groups of five, were presented with a catalog of equipment, cost data, and measuring instruments, and asked to develop a plan for a playground that would serve students in their school. Two facets were measured: the behavioral, which included motivation to accept the problem, commitment to the task, allocation of responsibility, and nature of group leadership; and the cognitive, which included four summary rating scores on identification of variables, measurement, calculation, and recording. Except for scores on identification of variables, where pretest scores were significantly higher than posttest scores, no significant differences were noted between pretests and posttests. Interviews disclosed that teachers perceived children in the USMES program to be more responsible for their own learning and to show growth in data collection abilities, in graphing skills, in hypothesis testing, and in communication with their peers. Although not supported by data, these

---

*That is, *humans.*

perceptions were consistent and persistent among teachers from all geographic and demographic areas involved in the program.

Shann (1975) and her colleagues again assessed the USMES program during the 1974–1975 school year, using the same behavioral, cognitive, and product scores as in the earlier study. No significant differences were found in behavioral scores comparing either pretest and posttest scores or in comparing USMES groups and controls. A significant increase in cognitive scores occurred with rising grade levels, but again without significant difference between experimental and control groups. Concern with the validity and reliability of the problem-solving instruments led to the development of a separate instrument (Shann, 1976) described earlier in the section on assessment (see page 16).

J. T. Bullock (1973) reported a study to determine the relative effectiveness of three different types of elementary school science curriculums in the development of selected problem-solving skills of sixth-grade students. The three curriculums were SAPA, the Laidlaw textbook series, and the Environmental Studies (ES) project materials. Bullock found that
• There was no significant difference between the problem-solving skills of students using the Laidlaw textbook series and those using SAPA.
• Students using the Laidlaw textbook series improved significantly more than those using ES materials.
• SAPA materials produced more improvement than did ES.
• Both SAPA and the textbook series led to significant improvement in problem-solving skills.

In a related study, F. D. Briet and J. T. Bullock (1974, April) assessed the long-term effectiveness of SAPA in the development of fifth and sixth graders' problem-solving skills. They compared certain problem-solving skills of children who had been in classrooms using the SAPA program for at least four years with the performance of children who had not used SAPA and found a significant difference in favor of the SAPA group.

Shaw (1978, 1983) attempted to determine the effect of the process-oriented science curriculum, SAPA II, on the ability of sixth graders to use the integrated process skills. He also tried to determine if problem solving learned in science would transfer to social studies, tested models concerning problem-solving skills to see if there were evidence for a hierarchy of such skills, and tried to find out if training in problem solving would increase students' proficiency in basic skills such as observing, inferring, and predicting. The experimental group scored higher than the controls on the problem-solving skills portions of both the science and social studies instruments, indicating that problem-solving skills can be taught by SAPA II and that these processes can transfer to social studies as well. Neither instrument showed significant differences between the groups for basic process skills, except that the experimental group scored higher than the controls on classification (in social studies but not in science). Only students who mastered the basic skills could also use the problem-solving skills, supporting the theory of a hierarchy—only students mastering the basic skills could become proficient in problem solving.

In most but not all cases, using inquiry-oriented curriculums produces significant gains in problem-solving skills, as well as gains in attitudes toward science. These gains vary, however, from one curriculum to another and from grade level to grade level. Yet, when we consider the total picture presented by the research, we find convincing evidence that the curriculum does make a difference. In short, using a curriculum designed to promote an inquiry approach *will* result in enhanced problem-solving abilities, as well as gains in other outcomes.

Practical Implications for Teaching Science

To summarize the research in science education on any topic in any area is to present a temporary structure, a snapshot of arrested time in a changing and growing enterprise. Thus, generalizations coming out of this summary are, of necessity, tentative and subject to change as the research base supporting them shifts and expands. The implications below do not relate to particular studies but are, instead, attempts to translate the various findings into suggestions for practical application.

- **Plan for and include process objectives in science instruction.** Problem-solving and science process skills are clearly related. Including instruction in science process skills will contribute to the development of problem-solving skills.

- **Include the assessment of problem-solving skills as part of evaluation in the science program.** While the existing instruments vary in validity and reliability, the information gained from assessment can aid in improving outcomes of science instruction.

- **Use multiple approaches to instruction.** It is clear that there are differences among learners in cognitive development and styles, learning preferences, and verbal and spatial abilities, among other things. Multiple instructional approaches provide more opportunities for learners with differing styles.

- **Provide practice in problem-solving activities.** Work at generating hunches or hypotheses, at identifying and controlling variables, at organizing data and processing information aids in the development of problem-solving ability. In addition, active involvement in inquiry and problem solving promotes positive attitudes toward and interest in science as well as contributing to gains in scientific knowledge.

- **Include concrete representations and hands-on experiences.** Few adolescents consistently operate at the formal operational level; many, in fact, reason below their capacity. In order to promote both problem-solving and cognitive development, offer concrete, manipulable experiences.

- **Use specific problem-solving strategies.** General strategies do not appear to be as useful as specific ones applied to concrete examples. Transfer of these skills seems to work best when the same procedures and equipment are used for new problems.

- **Start with familiar variables.** Beginning with the familiar influences students' ability to identify and control variables. Too much new content all at once can result in confusion.

- **Provide for student-structured learning and interaction among students.** A free-choice environment promotes gains in problem-solving ability. The interaction of team or group work also appears to contribute to gains.

- **Integrate conceptual and process objectives in the science program.** Achievement outcomes include both concepts and processes, and the benefits to students appear to be greater when content and processes are integrated over a long period of time rather than in a hurry.

- **Use science curriculum materials designed to promote inquiry and problem solving.** While there is variation in research findings, the overall results indicate that curricular materials designed to promote inquiry skills and problem solving do, in fact, produce increased abilities in those areas.

References

Berger, C. F. (1982). Attainment of skill in using science processes, I: Instrumentation, methodology, and analysis. *Journal of Research in Science Teaching, 19*(3), 249-260.

Berger, C. F., and Pintrich, P. R. (1986). Attainment of skill in using science processes, II: Grade and task effects. *Journal of Research in Science Teaching, 23*(8), 739-747.

Blosser, P. E. (1982). *Teaching science to middle school students* (Information Bulletin No. 2). Columbus, OH: ERIC Clearinghouse of Science, Mathematics, and Environmental Education, The Ohio State University.

Bowyer, J., Chen, B., and Thier, H. D. (1976). *A free-choice environment: Learning without instruction. Advancing education through science-oriented programs.* Berkeley: University of California, Lawrence Hall of Science. (ERIC Document Reproduction Service No. ED 182 166)

Briet, F. D., and Bullock, J. T. (1974, April). *The effectiveness of Science—A Process Approach [SAPA] in the development of problem-solving skills in fifth- and sixth-grade students.* Paper presented at the 47th annual meeting of the National Association for Research in Science Teaching, Chicago.

Brooks, E. T. (1982). The effects of mastery instruction on the learning and retention of science process skills (Doctoral dissertation, Indiana University). *Dissertation Abstracts International, 43,* 1103A.

Bullock, J. T. (1973). A comparison of the relative effectiveness of three types of elementary school science curricula in the development of problem-solving skills (Doctoral dissertation, University of Florida, 1972). *Dissertation Abstracts International, 34,* 185A.

Burns, J. C., Okey, J. R., and Wise, C. (1985). Development of an integrated process skill test: TIPS II. *Journal of Research in Science Teaching, 22*(2), 169-177.

Butts, D. P. (1964). The evaluation of problem solving in science. *Journal of Research in Science Teaching, 2*(2), 116-122.

Butts, D. P., and Jones, H. L. (1966). Inquiry training and problem solving in elementary school children. *Journal of Research in Science Teaching, 4*(1), 21-27.

Champagne, A. B., and Klopfer, L. E. (1977). A 60-year perspective on three issues in science education: I. Whose ideas are dominant? II. Representation of women. III. Reflective thinking and problem solving. *Science Education, 61*(4), 431-452.

Champagne, A. B., and Klopfer, L. E. (1981a, January). Problem solving as outcome and method in science teaching: Insights from 60 years of experience. *School Science and Mathematics, 81*(1), 3-8.

Champagne, A. B., and Klopfer, L. E. (1981b). Structuring process skills and the solution of verbal problems involving science concepts. *Science Education, 65*(5), 493-511.

Chiappetta, E. L., and Russell, J. M. (1982). The relationship among logical thinking, problem-solving instruction, and knowledge and application of Earth science subject matter. *Science Education, 66*(1), 85-93.

Coble, C. R. (1986, March). *A cooperative study of science attitudes and involvement in science activities of U.S. and Japanese middle-grade students.* Paper presented at the 59th annual meeting of the National Association for Research in Science Teaching, San Francisco.

Cox, D. A. H. (1981). Early adolescent use of selected problem-solving skills using microcomputers (Doctoral dissertation, University of Michigan, 1980). *Dissertation Abstracts International, 41,* 3855A.

Cronin, L., and Padilla, M. J. (1986, March). *The development of a middle grades integrated science process skills test.* Paper presented at the 59th annual meeting of the National Association for Research in Science Teaching, San Francisco.

Davis, M. (1979). The effectiveness of a guided-inquiry discovery approach in an elementary school science curriculum (Doctoral dissertation, University of Southern California, 1978). *Dissertation Abstracts International, 39,* 4164-A.

Dillashaw, F. G., and Okey, J.R. (1980). Test of the integrated science process skills for secondary science students. *Science Education, 64*(5), 601-608.

Dunlop, D. L., and Fazio, F. (1975, March). *A study of abstract preferences in problem-solving tasks and their relationship to abstract ability and formal thought.* Paper presented at the 48th annual meeting of the National Association for Research in Science Teaching, Los Angeles.

Egolf, K. L. (1979). The effects of two modes of instruction on students' abilities to solve quantitative word problems in science (Doctoral dissertation, University of Maryland, 1978). *Dissertation Abstracts International, 40,* 778A.

Foster, G. W. (1982, April). *Creativity and the group problem-solving process.* Paper presented at the 55th annual meeting of the National Association for Research in Science Teaching, Lake Geneva, WI.

Friot, F. E. (1971). The relationship between an inquiry-teaching approach and intellectual development (Doctoral dissertation, University of Oklahoma, 1970). *Dissertation Abstracts International, 31,* 5872A.

Fyffe, D. W. (1972). The development of test items for the integrated science processes: Formulating hypotheses and defining operationally (Doctoral dissertation, Michigan State University, 1971). *Dissertation Abstracts International, 32,* 6823A.

Gagne, R. M. (1965). Psychological issues in Science—A Process Approach [SAPA]. In *The psychological basis of Science—A Process Approach* (pp 1-10). Washington, DC: American Association for the Advancement of Science.

Glasson, G. E. (1989). The effects of hands-on and teacher demonstration laboratory methods on science achievement in relation to reasoning ability and prior knowledge. *Journal of Research in Science Teaching, 26*(2), 121-131.

Gudaitis, D. J. (1971). The effects of two seventh-grade science programs, *Interaction of Man and the Biosphere* and *Science is Explaining* on student attitudes, science processes, and critical thinking (Doctoral dissertation, New York University). *Dissertation Abstracts International, 32,* 1259A.

Helgeson, S. L., Blosser, P. E., and Howe, R. W. (1977). *The status of pre-college science, mathematics, and social science education: 1955-1975* (Vol. 1, Science education). Columbus: The Ohio State University, Center for Science and Mathematics Education.

Hurd, P. D. (1978). *Early adolescence: Perspectives and recommendations.* Washington, DC: National Science Foundation.

Jacknicke, K. G., and Pearson, D. A. (1979, March). *The influence of the reflective/ impulsive dimension on problem-solving skills in elementary school science.* Paper presented at the 52nd annual meeting of the National Association for Research in Science Teaching, Atlanta.

Johnson, R. T., and Johnson, D. W. (1989). Cooperative learning and the gifted science student. In P. F. Brandwein and A. H. Passow (Eds.), *Gifted young in science: Potential through performance* (pp. 321-329). Washington, DC: NSTA.

Jones, H. L. (1966). The development of a test of scientific inquiry, using the tab format, and an analysis of its relationship to selected student behaviors and abilities (Doctoral dissertation, University of Texas). *Dissertation Abstracts International, 27,* 415-A.

Jones, W. W. (1983). An investigation of the effect of acknowledging successful autonomous discovery by seventh-grade students exposed to the Inquiry Development Program (Doctoral dissertation, University of Northern Colorado, 1972). *Dissertation Abstracts International, 33,* 3425A.

Lawsiripaiboon, P. (1983). The effects of a problem-solving strategy on ninth-grade students' ability to apply and analyze physical science subject matter (Doctoral dissertation, University of Houston). *Dissertation Abstracts International, 44,* 1409A.

Lawson, A. E., and Wollman, W. T. (1977). Cognitive level, cognitive style, and value judgment. *Science Education, 61*(3), 397-407.

Linn, M. C., Clement, C., Pulos, S., and Sullivan, P. (1989). Scientific reasoning during adolescence: The influence of instruction in science knowledge and reasoning strategies. *Journal of Research in Science Teaching, 26*(2), 171-187.

Linn, M. C., and Levine, D. I. (1976). *Adolescent reasoning: The development of ability to control variables.* Berkeley: University of California, Lawrence Hall of Science. (ERIC Document Reproduction Service No. ED 182 164)

Linn, M. C., and Levine, D. I. (1977). Scientific reasoning ability in adolescence: Theoretical viewpoints and educational implications. *Journal of Research in Science Teaching, 14*(4), 371-384.

Malinka, R. M. (1981). The middle school: An operational definition. In D. V. Ochs (Ed.), *Improving practices in middle school science* (pp. 1-22). (1981 Association for the Education of Teachers in Science Yearbook.) Columbus: The Ohio State University, ERIC Clearinghouse for Science, Mathematics, and Environmental Education.

Mandell, A. (1980). Problem-solving strategies of sixth-grade students who are superior problem solvers. *Science Education, 64*(2), 203-211.

Mattheis, F. E., Coble, C. R., and Spooner, W. E. (1986, March). *A study of the logical thinking skills of junior high school students in North Carolina and Japan.* Paper presented at the 59th annual meeting of the National Association for Research in Science Teaching, San Francisco.

Mayer, V. J., and Richmond, J. M. (1982). An overview of assessment instruments in science. *Science Education, 66*(1), 49-66.

McKee, D. J. (1978, March). *A comparative study of problem-solving ability and confidence for sixth-grade science students exposed to two contrasting strategies.* Paper presented at the 51st annual meeting of the National Association for Research in Science Teaching, Ontario.

Norton, R. E. (1971). A developmental study in assessing children's ability to solve problems in science (Doctoral dissertation, University of Texas at Austin). *Dissertation Abstracts International, 33*, 204A.

Novak, J. D. (1989). The role of content and process in the education of science teachers. In P. F. Brandwein and A. H. Passow (Eds.), *Gifted young in science: Potential through performance* (pp. 307–320). Washington, DC: NSTA.

Novak, J. D., Gowin, G. B., and Johansen, G. T. (1983). The use of concept mapping and knowledge Vee mapping with junior high school students. *Science Education, 67*(5), 625–645.

Padilla, M. J., Okey, J. R., and Dillashaw, F. G. (1983). The relationship between science process skill and formal thinking abilities. *Journal of Research in Science Teaching, 20*(3), 239–246.

Padilla, M. J., Okey, J. R., and Garrard, K. (1984). The effects of instruction on integrated science process skill achievement. *Journal of Research in Science Teaching, 21*(3), 277–287.

Pouler, C. A. (1976). *The effect of intensive instruction in hypothesis generation upon the quantity and quality of hypotheses and the quantity and diversity of information search questions contributed by ninth-grade students* (Doctoral dissertation, University of Maryland). (ERIC Document Reproduction Service No. ED 128 225)

Pouler, C. A., and Wright, E. (1977, March). *The effect of intensive instruction in hypothesis generation upon hypothesis-forming and questioning behaviors of ninth-grade students.* Paper presented at the 50th annual meeting of the National Association for Research in Science Teaching, Cincinnati. (ERIC Document Reproduction Service No. ED 135 661)

Quinn, M. E., and George, K. D. (1975). Teaching hypothesis formation. *Science Education, 59*(3), 289–296.

Quinn, M. E., and Kessler, C. (1980, April). *Science education and bilingualism.* Paper presented at the 53rd annual meeting of the National Association for Research in Science Teaching, Boston.

Rakow, S. J. (1985). Excellence in school science. *School Science and Mathematics, 85*(8), 631–634.

Reynolds, K. E., Pitotti, N. W., Rakow, S. J., Thompson, T., and Wohl, S. (1984). *Excellence in middle school/junior high school science programs.* Washington, DC: NSTA.

Robison, R. W. (1974). The development of items which assess the processes of controlling variables and interpreting data (Doctoral dissertation, Michigan State University). *Dissertation Abstracts International, 35,* 1522A.

Ronning, R. R., and McCurdy, D. W. (1982). The role of instruction in the development of problem-solving skills in science. In R. E. Yager (Ed.), *What research says to the science teacher* (Vol. 4, pp. 31–41). Washington, DC: NSTA.

Ronning, R. R., McCurdy, D. W., and Ballinger, R. (1984). Individual differences: A third component in problem-solving instruction. *Journal of Research in Science Teaching, 21*(1), 71–82.

Ross, J. A., and Maynes, F. J. (1983a). Development of a test of experimental problem-solving skills. *Journal of Research in Science Teaching, 20*(1), 63–75.

Ross, J. A., and Maynes, F. J. (1983b). Experimental problem solving: An instructional improvement field experiment. *Journal of Research in Science Teaching, 20*(6), 543–556.

Rudnitsky, A. N., and Hunt, C. R. (1986). Children's strategies for discovering cause–effect relationships. *Journal of Research in Science Teaching, 23*(5), 451–464.

Russell, J. M. (1979). The effects of problem solving on junior high school students' ability to apply and analyze earth science subject matter (Doctoral dissertation, University of Houston). *Dissertation Abstracts International, 40,* 1386A.

Russell, J. M., and Chiappetta, E. L. (1980, April). *The effects of problem solving on the achievement of Earth science students as measured with Bloom's Taxonomy.* Paper presented at the 53rd annual meeting of the National Association for Research in Science Teaching, Boston.

Russell, J. M., and Chiappetta, E. L. (1981). The effects of a problem-solving strategy on the achievement of Earth science students. *Journal of Research in Science Teaching, 18*(4), 295–301.

Saunders, W. L., and Jesunathadas, J. (1988). The effect of task content upon proportional reasoning. *Journal of Research in Science Teaching, 25*(1), 59–67.

Scott, N. C., Jr. (1973). Cognitive style and inquiry strategy: A five-year study. *Journal of Research in Science Teaching, 10*(4), 323–330.

Schlenker, G. C. (1971). The effects of an inquiry development program on elementary school children's science learning (Doctoral dissertation, New York University, 1970). *Dissertation Abstracts International, 32,* 104A.

Schmiess, E. G. (1971). An investigative approach to elementary school science teaching

---

(Doctoral dissertation, University of North Dakota, 1970). *Dissertation Abstracts International, 31*, 4391A.

Shann, M. H. (1975). *An evaluation of unified science and mathematics for elementary schools (USMES) during the 1973-1974 school year.* Boston: Boston University. (ERIC Document Reproduction Service No. ED 135 861)

Shann, M. H. (1976). *Measuring problem-solving skills and processes in elementary school children.* Boston: Boston University, School of Education. (ERIC Document Reproduction Service No. ED 135 807)

Shann, M. H., Reali, N. C., Bender, H., Aiello, T., and Hench, L. (1975). *Student effects of an interdisciplinary curriculum for real problem solving: The 1974-1975 USMES Evaluation. Final report.* Boston: Boston University. (ERIC Document Reproduction Service No. ED 135 864)

Shaw, T. J. (1978). The effects of problem-solving training in science upon utilization of problem-solving skills in science and social studies (Doctoral dissertation, Oklahoma State University, 1977). *Dissertation Abstracts International, 38*, 5227A.

Shaw, T. J. (1982). *ORES—Objective referenced evaluation in science.* Manhattan, KS: Kansas State University. (ERIC Document Reproduction Service No. ED 037 698)

Shaw, T. J. (1983). The effect of a process-oriented science curriculum upon problem-solving ability. *Science Education, 67*(5), 615-623.

Spooner, W. E. (1986, March). *An assessment of integrated process skills of junior high school students.* Paper presented at the 59th annual meeting of the National Association for Research in Science Teaching, San Francisco.

Staver, J. R. (1984). Research on formal reasoning patterns in science education: Some messages for science teachers. *School Science and Mathematics, 84*(7), 573-589.

Staver, J. R. (1986). The effects of problem format, number of independent variables, and their interaction on student performance on a control-of-variables reasoning problem. *Journal of Research in Science Teaching, 23*(6), 533-542.

Tannenbaum, R. S. (1969). The development of [the] Test of Science Processes (Doctoral dissertation, Columbia University, 1968). *Dissertation Abstracts International, 29*, 2159A.

Tobin, K. G., and Capie, W. (1981). The development and validation of a group test of logical thinking. *Educational and Psychological Measurement, 41*(2), 413-423.

White, E. P. (1978). Problem solving: Its history as a focus in curriculum development. *School Science and Mathematics, 78*(3), 183-188.

Wilson, J. T. (1973, March). *An investigation into the effects of generating hunches upon subsequent search activities in problem-solving situations.* Paper presented at the 46th annual meeting of the National Association for Research in Science Teaching, Detroit. (ERIC Document Reproduction Service No. ED 079 064)

Witkin, H. A., Oltman, P. K., Raskin, E., and Karp, S. A. (1971). Group embedded figures test. Palo Alto, CA: Consulting Psychologists Press.

Wright, E. (1978). The influence of intensive instruction upon the open exploration behavior of ninth-grade students. *Journal of Research in Science Teaching, 15*(6), 535-541.

Problem Solving in Earth Science Education

Charles R. Ault, Jr.
Lewis and Clark College
Portland, Oregon

Why are problems in Earth science important? Men and women in many disciplines have contributed to our present understanding of the Earth as a body in space with properties that reflect its long and eventful history. The Earth sciences teach that our home planet has been a very different place than it is today, that change is the norm and permanence an illusion. But present patterns are in a balance that is more precarious than at any previous time in the Earth's history. Squarely within this balance are the possibilities of nuclear destruction and environmental contamination. Our actions can tip the balance. Students ought to become accustomed to thinking about change on a scale that was once unthinkable.

Within this overarching theme of change in time and space are the various phenomena addressed by problem solving in Earth science. Students can learn to predict weather, interpret celestial motions and events, calculate rates of stream discharge, evaluate the economic benefits and environmental costs of using Earth's resources, assess geologic hazards, extrapolate climatic trends, understand coastal change, and model oceanic systems. Most of these phenomena are incompletely understood and only partially observed by most people.

The challenge of problem solving in Earth science is to connect the global scale to everyday experience, to simplify complex events into patterns amenable to problem-solving conventions, such as geometric analysis of rock structures; contour maps of temperature, pressure, and moisture conditions in air masses; and orbital models of celestial motions. Opportunities in the field arise from the rich and readily available store of everyday problems to be solved. Difficulties include the interdisciplinary nature of solutions to these complex problems, which often demand knowledge of physics, chemistry, and biology.

The Nature of Problems in Earth Science

Some educators argue that problems in Earth science cannot be approached meaningfully without concepts and problem-solving skills from the three "basic" science disciplines. Others counter that the immediate presence of the sky, land, water, and air makes it possible to connect students' interest and awareness to scientific understanding without elaborate preparation. The next several paragraphs survey examples of phenomena addressed by Earth science. Their explanations often take the form of highly probable stories assembled over generations and after much scholarly debate. Each story is persuasive, and given the assembled, though still incomplete, data, very likely true. Each addresses change on a scale difficult to imagine.

Scablands. The change in the landscape of western Washington state from a plateau of basalt to a corrugated washboard of hills (the Scablands) occurred in a geologic flash, presumably when an ice dam broke. This physical change dwarfs in scale virtually all other instances of fluid-etched ripples on continental rock and helps to interpret landforms on the surface of Mars.

Red Giants. The Sun has burned yellow-hot for millennia of millenia. Should it exhaust its primary fuel, hydrogen, and switch to producing energy by fusing larger nuclei, the pressures generated would propel its outer gaseous shell as far as the Earth's orbit. At least, the size and brilliance of Red Giants like Antares suggest it would.

"Normal" Weather. Each night on the local news a weather forecaster gives the "normal" temperature for that date. What is normal weather for a day? Weather means constant change in atmospheric conditions. Over time, patterns in weather yield a definable climate for a region. But the notion of there being a normal pattern or a day with normal temperatures is misleading. The variations we expect depend on our time scale. Snow in July in New England is unexpected on an annual time scale. Does that mean that snow in New England is not normal on a millennial time scale? Perhaps every 10 centuries or so a July snowfall in the Connecticut River Valley is a good bet, just as a tornado in winter is normal every decade or so in Missouri.

Catastrophe. Environmental policy dilemmas, conflicting risk management theories, and seemingly endless scientific debates abound in the Earth sciences because the data are never complete. Typical problems, such as the "demise of the dinosaurs," even when rephrased more scientifically as the "scale of comparative extinction rates across diverse taxonomic groups at the end of Cretaceous time," have no resolutions, only shifting degrees of consensus. Risk management assessments about numbers of deaths in the coal mining industry per unit of BTU production versus projected deaths from nuclear power mishaps are bound to provoke disagreement, especially in the wake of the Chernobyl disaster.

Imaging

Those who teach Earth science strongly believe that the visual dimension is essential if science is to be meaningful and useful for solving real-world problems. Earth processes are easier to envision than those of chemistry and physics—if we can cope with the problem of scale. Picture the ancient moon on the horizon, much larger than it appears to us today. Imagine the sweep of tides much grander than those that now circle the globe. Apply some physics, at least a notion of the conservation of angular momentum, and deduce the number of days there would be in a year if the moon were closer. Taken together, these images provide the solution to a fossil puzzle: why daily growth cycles on fossil corals from hundreds of millions of years ago suggest 400 or more days per year. But the fossil coral/moon tide/days-in-a-year puzzle has a solution that is not obvious on the human scale of change, of time, and of space.

Instructors agree that students must develop skills in visualization to solve problems in Earth science. What makes visualization difficult is the need to scale a set of incomplete observations into a workable schema to which Earth science problem-solving conventions may be applied. As diverse as the Earth sciences are, the problem domains of all of them are characterized by great scale, incomplete or indirect observation of complex systems, and limited conventions for visual representation of problem situations.

Regrettably, there is little tradition of research into the nature of learning and problem solving in this seemingly intractable context. Some notable studies, however, show how students reason about the Earth as a body in space (Nussbaum, 1979, June; Sneider and Pulos, 1983, April), infer geologic relationships (Ault, 1982, November), and apply the hydrologic cycle (Stevens and Collins, 1980). Theorists in general education have examined learning in Earth science as well, because it is a subject commonly taught to adolescents. Those theorists have been interested in instructional variables (Russell and Chiapetta, 1981, July), application of the philosophy of science to curriculum structure (Finley, 1981, October; 1982, November), or the nature of cognitive processes (Champagne and Klopfer, 1981, October; Novak, Gowin, and Johansen, 1983).

The following sections of this paper sum up findings and insights from each of these areas. Examples of phenomena in Earth science amenable to a problem-solving approach to curriculum planning follow this summary of recent research. The paper ends with a general set of recommendations and speculation on fruitful possibilities for future research.

Reasoning About Earth in Space

Most students believe that the Earth orbits the Sun. They seldom recognize patterns in the change of position of celestial objects on an hourly, daily, weekly, monthly, or annual basis. And they seldom interpret these changes in terms of an orbital model—one involving a movable observer on a spinning sphere (the Earth) that circles another sphere (the Sun) while the planets orbit the Sun at rates proportional to their distance from the center. Other objects (the stars) are so distant that their position appears unchanged on the scale of human lifetimes and at the distance of everyday observation. Information about the orbital model and facility with language about it often overlie a residual intuitive model of a flat Earth, even for adolescents (Nussbaum, 1979, June).

The tradition of research on Earth and gravity concepts began with J. Nussbaum and J. D. Novak's 1976 interview study of 26 second graders. Interviewers probed children's notions of the path a falling object might take when dropped from different locations on the Earth. Props included globes and picture cards of the Earth as seen from space. Even children who viewed the Earth as spherical with people everywhere clung to a notion of "absolute down." According to this notion, if objects could keep falling through the Earth, they would end up at the South Pole, not the center of the Earth.

Nussbaum (1979, June) reported that Israeli students' notions of absolute down persisted through grade eight. C. A. Klein (1982) found common levels of naive thinking about the Earth in space across Mexican-American and Anglo-American cultural groups. G. Mali and A. Howe (1979) concluded from interviews with Nepalese children that cultural differences strongly influenced performance on five Earth motion tasks adapted from those used by Nussbaum and Novak. Task I consisted of questions about the shape and position of the Earth in space and an observer's orientation on Earth. Task II dealt with the path of a falling stone at various locations on the globe. Task III posed the problem of how water in corked and uncorked jars would respond to gravity at places around the world. Task IV featured seven persons stationed around the globe. Each dropped a stone, and students predicted its path (similar to number II). In Task V, students indicated on diagrams how a stone might fall if there were tunnels through the Earth through which it might fall. The basic notions explored were the sphericity of the Earth and the action of gravitational force towards the center of the Earth for all surface locations. However, in a comprehensive summary and rigorous replication of this research tradition, C. Sneider and S. Pulos (1983, April) reexamined the cross-cultural data, finding little support for the hypothesis that cultural differences affect development of children's concepts about the Earth as a cosmic sphere with "down" being towards its center and the direction of Earth's gravity. Within-age-group differences were more substantial than those between cultural groups. Sneider and Pulos did validate the basic Nussbaum scheme of levels (see figure) for the Earth motion.

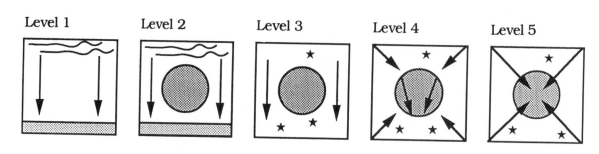

Figure redrawn from Sneider and Pulos' diagram (1983), which was published in *Science Education*, 67(2), p. 206; that figure was in turn based on one by J. Nussbaum printed in the same journal, Vol. 63(1), p. 83. Redrawn figure copyright© 1979, 1983, appears by permission of John Wiley and Sons.

However, Sneider and Pulos distinguished more carefully than had Nussbaum between notions of the Earth's shape and understandings of the direction of gravitational acceleration.

C. R. Ault, Jr., (1986a) critiqued Sneider and Pulos' paper and pointed out additional unanswered questions raised by this line of inquiry. For example, do individuals hold incompatible views from two levels simultaneously? In what way is the particular concept of gravitational up and down related to general comprehension of changing frames of reference?

With a good mental model of orbital motion—an Earth concept at level five in the Nussbaum scheme—students can attack questions such as "Will a Brazilian see the same moon phase tonight as a Canadian? When does the Sun shine on the south wall of a home in Sydney, Australia? How can shadows be used to prove which direction is north for someone in Ohio?" However, even many college-age students are not prepared to think on this level. L. J. G. Kelsey (1980) determined that most students in a general, introductory astronomy course could not reason properly about projective space. She presented six problems to the students:
• coordinating perspectives of mountains
• coordinating perspectives of stars in the sky
• recognizing distortions due to planar rotation and projection
• interpreting lunar phases from a person-centered frame of reference
• interpreting lunar phases from an Earth-centered model
• interpreting lunar phases from a two-dimensional Earth, Moon, Sun diagram
So few students were successful in the sixth area that Kelsey eliminated the category from her final report. Her work and the Nussbaum tradition suggest how tenaciously students may hold to intuitive notions gleaned from everyday perspectives to the detriment of reasoning about the Earth in space. Lightman and Sadler (1988) have underscored this conclusion in their delightful essay, "The Earth is *Round?* Who Are You Kidding?," which summarizes the cosmic up and down literature for teachers.

Reasoning About Geological Relationships

Using data from the Learning in Science Project and a New Zealand study described by R. Osborne and P. Freyberg (1985), J. C. Happs (1982a, b, c, d) reported exhaustively on students' views of phenomena in Earth science. From his findings, he drew implications for teaching about rocks and minerals, glaciers, soils, and mountains from middle- through secondary-school levels.

From interviews and sorting tasks, Happs concluded (1982c) that children's typical approach to constructing categories for rock and mineral samples contrasted sharply with the approach likely for Earth scientists. For example, students ages 11 through 17 were asked to sort a collection of rocks and minerals according to common properties. Students discussing their decisions rarely used the term *mineral*, preferring to call all objects *rocks*. *Stones* referred to small pieces of rock, a major subcategory. The students used *crystal* and *pebble* frequently, but in nonscientific ways. Weight and shape were the attributes most commonly used for identification. The students made little connection between minerals and the fabric of rocks. Older students used a mixture of everyday and scientific schemes for classifying specimens: *sedimentary, ordinary,* and *exotic,* for example.

Children in the Learning in Science Project described what they noticed about pictures of glaciated landforms (Happs, 1982a). Interviews probed children's ideas concerning the process that had shaped these landforms. The children were unaware that glaciers tended to move, were bodies of ice, and produced major erosional features. Instead the students imagined glaciers as "always there" and made no association between fluctuating climate and glacial movement, if they had any awareness of glacial movement at all. They made no link between U-shaped valleys, fjords, moraines, and the erosional work of glaciers. Some thought the valleys resulted from old volcanoes.

Investigating students' grasp of mountain building processes, Happs (1982b) found that two-thirds of his sample of 37 were not aware that a dormant volcano might erupt again. Eighty percent of the New Zealand students he interviewed could not relate mountain building in their nation to plate tectonics. Mountain building and glaciation should have particular relevance to New Zealanders, who live in an active plate margin zone. Happs judged the absence of any appreciation of tectonic concepts among a majority of adolescents a disturbing situation.

Another Happs study (1982d) concluded that students had little sense of soil formation processes or the dynamic environmental factors related to soil change over time. He urged teachers to emphasize time-dependent properties of soils. Many adolescents in the Happs study held a notion of simple cycling between soil and clay: Soil changes to clay, clay to rock, rock to soil.

M. R. Cohen (1968) used a "mudpile mountain" to assess upper elementary-grade children's grasp of fluvial processes in a microgeology context. Water running down the dirt pile created gullies. Small lakes formed when the flow was blocked. Cohen asked children to predict the future of the lake and to justify their predictions in terms of processes that could make the lake larger or smaller, deeper or more shallow. He also asked his subjects how runoff water might sort dirt at the bottom of the gully. Their pre-instruction predictions varied widely. Afterward, nearly all grasped a simple principle of transport: Water carries small particles farther from the slope than large ones.

Cohen's work, which antedated Happs' studies by more than a decade, underscores the value of listening to how children explain everyday events in their own terms. Happs reminds us to presume very little about what adolescents know before instruction in Earth science. Research with young children (Donaldson, 1982) suggests that logical reasoning improves when the reason for asking a child a question and the question itself fit purposes that have meaning to the child. There is no reason to discount the importance of either Happs' or M. Donaldson's conclusions when teaching students of any age.

Curriculum materials should illustrate abstract ideas with everyday objects. When reasoning about temporal order and duration in terms of everyday experience, for instance, children's logic parallels that of geologists attempting to solve problems about the relative ages of rocks. Children's concepts about time present no barrier to understanding the geologic past; however, their lack of knowledge about geologic objects and events leads to confused, contradictory thinking (Ault, 1982, November). When provided with clear plastic tubes containing layers of trash, sampled from different positions in an imaginary garbage pile, 20 children from grades 4 and 6 had no difficulty inferring an overall sequence of layers from top to bottom. They simply matched or correlated portions of one tube with another, allowing for possible thinning or thickening of a layer. Some even surmised that grass layers, repeated on a weekly basis, reflected weekend yard work. In this context, children easily isolated age cues: Position indicated how long ago, relatively speaking, a type of garbage was deposited. Perhaps, as some suggested, the stuff was "already old"; they pointed to torn pieces of last month's newspaper as an example.

But when presented with diagrams of rock columns from local roadsides and park gorges, the same children were unable to reason consistently about relative ages of rocks. They used cues such as crumbliness, color, compaction, and hardness to evaluate the possible age of a rock without considering its position in the column. Consider the analogous confusion for the geologist: very ancient igneous rock redeposited as sediments in a conglomerate above another rock. The result is a young mixture of very old fragments. Is the "age" the age of the rocks making the conglomerate or the time passed since the coarse sediment was deposited? In one sense, old rock lies above a younger layer. In terms of layering (or dispositional events), there is no ambiguity: Recent lies above. Students who solve problems involving reasoning about relative age must attend carefully to the precise meanings of "age." They must sort the relative time age cues from the aging process cues and keep straight about what events a time question actually asks (Ault, 1982, November).

Reasoning About the Water Cycle

Perhaps the most interesting everyday problem many students tackle in Earth science is weather prediction. They can match their skills against those of the evening weather forecaster on television. But weather prediction involves data gathering and interpretation on several different scales. First, a forecaster must observe local temperature, humidity, air pressure, cloud cover and type, visibility, wind speed and direction (at the surface and above), dew point temperature, and thermal inversions. For the full picture, though, a forecaster needs similar information from many other localities. While keen observation of cloud type, wind direction, humidity, and short-term temperature change might eventually enable a student to make reliable forecasts, local observation cannot constitute a full explanation of weather change.

Gathering of data on a large scale permits the mapping of pressure and temperature contours, wind circulation, and air mass distribution. Cloud cover, storms, wind direction change, and temperature and humidity patterns then can be seen as the results of interacting masses of air, each with characteristics based on where the masses originally came into relative equilibrium with the Earth's surface (polar land, tropical sea, etc.). In these examples the data is straightforward and simple, though the system being represented is complex beyond complete prediction—a situation typifying problems in Earth science.

Comprehending complex systems requires elaborate, even multiple, conceptual models (Stevens and Collins, 1980). Teaching aimed at bringing about such

understanding involves probing a student's surface errors for possible deeper misconceptions, then guiding instruction according to correction strategies. According to A. L. Stevens and A. Collins, such diagnosis and correction require
• knowledge of common student errors and the relationship of such errors to misconceptions
• understanding of the types of real-world, experiential knowledge students use to comprehend novel problems
• understanding of various ways to apply such real-world knowledge

In a study of students' understanding of rainfall, Stevens and Collins pursued these issues. Characterizing learning as a process of refining mental models into better correspondence with the world, they identified four models for rainfall used by lay people or explained in textbooks: a "simulation" model of evaporation, a "functional" model of evaporation, a water-cycle model, and a climate model.
• The simulation model is based on imagery of water as discrete, moving, colliding, and attracting/repelling particles. This model accounts for evaporation in terms of particle escape from the liquid phase.
• In the functional model, evaporation is associated with the amount of heat; escape rate becomes the focus of attention and a function of water temperature in sophisticated versions of this model.
• The water cycle model connects evaporation and precipitation. In its sophisticated version, air masses play critical roles; in its rudimentary form, clouds are central.
• The climate model, similar in most respects to the water cycle, represents a large-scale, geographical perspective. This last model incorporates water and air currents around the world that interact with land masses.

Stevens and Collins find profound educational implications in these models. They suggest that multiple models should be taught explicitly as alternative points of view about a topic. The emphasis should be on the kinds of situations and problems for which each model is applicable and on how to apply them to solve different types of novel problems. At the same time, students should learn the limitations of each model and how to test a solution derived from one model against another. Students might also be taught how various distortions of a model lead to different misconceptions, and how any model can be systematically refined to increase the accuracy of predictions based on it (p. 196).

Stevens and Collins' work on conceptual models grew out of their attempts to build computer tutors according to "expert systems" programming conventions (with numerous if-then rules as subroutines). Expert systems are computer programs composed from exhaustive lists of rule statements crafted to resemble principles that govern an expert's thinking in a well-defined context. Queries posed to the expert system yield a decision, once sufficient input has been made to activate the network of rules satisfactorily. Typically, the system prompts for the inputs it needs to turn on or "fire" rules until a conclusion is reached. See B. G. Buchanan and E. H. Shortlifte (1984/1985). At a less formal level of description, J. Stepans and C. Kuehn (1985, September) conducted interviews with children in grades two and five on such weather phenomena as wind, clouds, thunder, lightning, rain, snow, and rainbows. Some children in both grades failed to use true causal explanations to account for these phenomena. In general, however, children who experienced hands-on science instruction gave causal answers more frequently than did those who learned school science from textbooks only.

Sometimes textbooks are actually misleading—as in the case of cross-sectional diagrams depicting underground water as a stripe of pure blue. Such an illustration only reinforces children's naive conception of underground water as subterranean lakes and caverns filled with clear water. This image may be accurate in regions with carbonate bedrock, but is highly misleading for most aquifers, saturated ground, buried gravel beds, and permeable bedrock. In addition to holding a lake-like image of underground water, most students have never considered the relationship between the water table and stream or lake surface levels. They are likely to imagine water-filled ditches and basins far above the level of the actual water table. Problems on recharging aquifers, functioning of wells, and how streams flow when surface runoff stops make no sense to someone reasoning from a naive conception of underground water.

It is seldom possible to observe underground water directly. This is the case with many of the phenomena studied in Earth science. Small-scale experiments may illustrate what happens on true scales, but only by analogy. Still, analogies that resolve dilemmas may prove reliable. Adding water to buckets of variously sized gravel to measure "empty spaces" may help to teach the concept of pore space and resolve a common dilemma: "What holds the rock above the water table up? If an underground lake supports the rock, why doesn't the pressure of the rock above squirt the water back up through the cracks it came down by?"

The idea of water under pressure can account for the flow of some springs. But solutions to complex problems involving underground water must integrate the concept of hydrostatic pressure with that of rock permeability. A naive image of underground lakes is a poor place to begin.

Instructional Variables and Promoting Problem Solving in Teaching Earth Science

A significant study of Earth-science-learning from a problem-solving perspective was done by J. M. Russell and E. L. Chiapetta (1981, July) and Chiapetta and Russell (1982, January), who used a model of problem solving in several parts: problem presentation, collection of relevant information, analysis of information, and production of a solution. The investigators assigned 287 students at random to 14 sections of Earth science. Seven sections received conventional instruction and seven experienced modifications emphasizing problem solving. The investigators randomly chose to study 70 students from the experimental sections and 70 from the conventional ones.

Teachers of the conventional sections asked questions almost entirely at the knowledge and comprehension levels of Bloom's Taxonomy (1956) and led laboratory exercises intended to confirm classroom concepts. Teachers of the problem-solving sections asked questions at the application and analysis levels of the Taxonomy. They conducted laboratory exercises using the researchers' three-part model. First, they presented a problem situation such as the following: A farmer was puzzled that apparently similar fields differed in irrigation needs and flooding tendencies. Next, students performed soil tests for porosity and permeability. Finally, they assumed the role of agricultural consultants and analyzed the data to solve the flooding and irrigation puzzle.

Russell and Chiapetta reached two important conclusions. First, logical thinking (or "intellectual competence" as measured by a 10-item Piagetian test) exerted greater influence on achievement than did instructional style. However, after accounting for intellectual competence among all students, the problem-solving treatment did lead to improved achievement on a 20-item test, especially at the higher levels of Bloom's Taxonomy.

Even studies that attempt no instructional intervention have the potential to inform teaching practice. L. J. Solarte (1984) attempted to model cognitive complexity to generate a guide for matching subject matter to cognitive ability. His study involved 433 Regents Earth science students in western New York. He concluded that such a scheme is feasible and could encourage teachers to adjust instruction.

D. A. Wiley (1984) contrasted the ability of two groups of ninth-grade students involved in field trip activities to develop abstract geological concepts. One group, which participated in a process-oriented field trip, was provided a guidebook that posed questions requiring inquiry. A similar number of students went on a content-oriented field trip carrying a guidebook containing direct information. Results showed that students using the process treatment developed long-lasting concrete concepts. Also in this work, Wiley determined that the "order of concept revelation" greatly influenced the development of lasting abstract concepts. Wiley's results echoed the findings of B. S. Thomas' (1968) research with 143 eighth graders taking Earth science. Thomas found a guided discovery teaching method superior to didactic techniques for helping high- and low-ability students gain inquiry, critical thinking, and problem-solving skills. However, didactic teaching was a better method than guided discovery in helping students achieve factual and conceptual knowledge.

In contrast to Thomas' findings, J. J. Monk and W. M. Stallings (1975, April) failed to find any differences between the scores of students who took factually oriented quizzes and those whose quizzes stressed application and analysis. In their study, the subjects were 200 undergraduates in a physical geography course. It may be that differences in achievement based on instructional treatment are more difficult to document in an older, more homogeneous population.

In 1984, J. S. Monk attempted to distinguish differences in the daily achievement patterns of students who had been classified as tending to operate cognitively at a formal or concrete level as they learned the abstract concept of plate tectonics. He found, as expected, that the students classified as formal reasoners outperformed concrete-level students. (V. J. Mayer and M. J. Kozlow [1980] had previously determined that daily measurement of eighth-grade students' learning about crustal evolution did not interfere with established classroom routines.)

S. L. Ulerick (1982) emphasizes how dependent beginning geology students are on their prior knowledge—as opposed to teacher guidance—as a means of integrating information from lectures, readings, and laboratories. Ulerick tested students' performance at three levels: literal knowledge, integration of knowledge, and transfer of knowledge. Students performed well only on the literal-knowledge level. Students with relevant prior information specific to higher-level questions did the best on integration and transfer. Teachers' directions for student study before a test emphasizing synthesis had no effect.

Even when an innovative instructional approach intended to engage students in inquiry or problem-solving processes achieves no greater effects on concept learning than does conventional instruction, student attitudes toward the subject may improve (Kern and Carpenter, 1984). Field-oriented, on-site problems are natural to an Earth science curriculum, but they do demand extra teaching effort, according to E. L. Kern and J. R. Carpenter. Not surprisingly, students who elect to take additional Earth science courses beyond a required introductory offering tend to exhibit low anxiety about the subject (Westerback, Gonzalez, and Primavera, 1984, December).

Despite lower anxiety among students electing further study in a field, they may encounter a course reputed to function as a screening mechanism. Organic chemistry has probably discouraged a few pre-med students; structural geology often frustrates prospective geology majors.

In a preliminary effort to characterize how students of structural geology reason, Ault (1986b) focused on "thickness problems." (Thickness problems present the student with the task of inferring the true thickness of a rock unit from measurement of its expression at the surface of the Earth.) A case-study approach led to think-aloud, problem-solving sessions with four students. Each student attempted to work through a self-generated hierarchy of thickness problems. Increase in difficulty of thickness problems conformed to the degree and number of departures from perpendicular intersections among three planes and one line of interest: the bed surface, the slope surface, an imaginary horizontal surface (map plane), and the traverse line across the bed exposure. Confusion of apparent with true dips (angles from the horizontal to bearings on surfaces) constrained the performance on these problems of students of structural geology, as suggested by a preliminary, qualitative analysis of the transcripts. Students might do better if they adopted as a goal a diagram describing their eventual solution and labeled the initial problem drawing and each subproblem phase with as complete a set of verbal phrases as possible (e.g., "This line is the bearing of the line of intersection on the bed surface with the slope surface in the map view or horizontal plane"). In short, precise verbal restatements describing the problem situation mediate spatial reasoning.

Learning Theory and Cognitive Process in Earth Science

F. N. Finley (1981, October; 1982, November) studied student mastery of geologic classification from the perspective of philosophy of science and an interest in geology subject matter in its own right. He found that the classification schemes themselves are context-bound to content. Methods for defining membership may be "classificatory" (characteristic present or not), comparative (ordinal judgments of more or less of an attribute), quantitative (real number value assigned to each element), or some combination of these three. In some respects, Finley's work resembles that of Stevens and Collins (1980) on multiple models of the water cycle, for Finley has found psychological profit in conceptual analysis of content.

Geologic classification uses mineral composition as a primary identifier of igneous rocks. Finley contrasted what was considered a simple scheme with a more sophisticated one, finding that the former used comparative characteristics and the latter quantitative ones. In addition, the simpler scheme lacked defining values, preventing students from applying "rules" for placing rocks in classes. Finley hypothesized that the ambiguity in the supposedly simpler scheme could create problems for students using it. Instructors employing supposedly "simpler" schemes need to provide values that can be used to define classes.

Finley and E. L. Smith (1980a, July) argued that the teacher should provide guidance in the initial solution of problems, even when the task uses a single-characteristic classification scheme. They argue that "task-specific strategies" are a type of knowledge. They analyzed in depth two task-specific strategies of sorting rocks according to relative grain size, or number of light-colored grains, or both. For example, Finley and Smith asked students to place rock samples in proper matrix cells according to column only (amount of light-colored grains) or to use row (grain size) and column descriptors. Finley and Smith's work treats concepts learned (such as rock properties) as information for decision making. Finally, Finley and Smith (1980b, November) stress that learning "conceptually related tasks" (such as tasks that pertain to classifying igneous rocks in particular, not classification in general) contributes to success on a complex, related task.

Following Finley and Smith's suggestions, A. B. Champagne and L. E. Klopfer (1981, October) attempted to explain the distinctive contributions of semantic knowledge (what concepts mean) and processing skills (strategies or procedures to follow) to solving problems successfully. Champagne and Klopfer examined student performance on two types of verbal problems: analogy and set membership. The problems treated the same subject matter, but differed in the processing skills needed for a solution. In the analogy problems, students picked a word from a short list (such as metamorphic, marble, sandstone, sedimentary) to complete an analogy (such as shale is to slate as limestone is to _____). In the set membership problems, students crossed out a word they believed did not belong with the other three (such as the word "volcano" in the list volcano, igneous, metamorphic, sedimentary). These problems had in common the requirement that students induce a structure relating the parts.

Champagne and Klopfer hypothesized that students displaying greater skills on structuring tasks would do better on the set-membership problems than those less able to display structuring skills. Champagne and Klopfer assessed such skills with the Concept Structuring Analysis Technique (ConSAT) (Champagne, Klopfer, Squires, and Desena, 1981). While being observed by means of the ConSAT technique, students arranged a small set of concept cards according to their thoughts about the words. The students explained their arrangements to an interviewer. In this instance, the two tasks were to arrange sets of cards into two categories, ROCK and MINERAL. Each set consisted of about 15 cards labeled with a single word, such as *slate, magma, graphite, calcite*, or with general terms, such as *rock, mineral, inorganic, solid substances, sedimentary*. Champagne and Klopfer found that students who rated high in the structuring process skill—those able to order semantic knowledge—scored high on set membership problems after instruction in rock classification. However, after a year no correlation could be found. Champagne and Klopfer also concluded that processing skill did not contribute significantly to analogy problem solving.

Researchers at Cornell also have worked on how processes learned for structuring knowledge transfer to problem-solving performance (Novak and Gowin, 1984). Novak, D. B. Gowin, and G. T. Johansen (1983, October) claimed that "concept mapping" and "Vee mapping" were helpful strategies for improving student knowledge achievement and problem-solving performance. The point of mapping exercises is to guide students in making their own knowledge explicit. Mapping practice helps students organize what they know for efficient application, find gaps in their understanding, and raise questions about how to improve their own understanding (Ault, 1985, September/October). Because the Cornell tradition of concept-mapping values has students take their own knowledge as an object of study in its own right, this approach has close links to traditions examining naive conceptions, alternative frameworks, and preinstructional knowledge.

Like Champagne and Klopfer, the Cornell researchers have concerned themselves with how the ability to structure knowledge may transfer to problem-solving performance. Novak (1977, 1989) believes that effective use of knowledge presupposes its organization hierarchically as displayed on a concept map. Whether the topic is oceans, moon phases, or continents, maps have a focus or superordinate concept, propositional or prepositional relationships, and concrete examples of key concepts. Maps depict layers of abstractions.

The desire to compare students' transfer of learning to problem solving led Novak, Gowin, and Johansen to devise a problem in which measures other than concept maps could be used to evaluate performance. They reported the results of a "wine bottle test." Four classes of eighth-grade students received instruction on solids, liquids, gases, and the gas laws. Each student attempted to explain why the cork popped out of an empty wine bottle that was placed in sunlight on a window sill after a night in a cold refrigerator. Students in two control classes answered only in essay form. Students in two experimental classes constructed concept maps from their original paragraphs and then rewrote the maps in paragraph form. Reviewers scored answers according to the number of valid relationships cited—for example, "Air expands when warmed." Students in experimental classes composed more than twice as many valid relationships as control students did.

Another team (Rollins, Denton, and Janke, 1983, November/December), working with many of the same assumptions about learning as the Cornell group, returned to D. L. Janke and M. D. Pella's 1972 concept list for grades K–12 to distill a nucleus of essential Earth science concepts for assessing the environmental, Earth, and astronomical knowledge of Texas high school seniors. This team investigated how well students could select examples of given concepts and identify related ones. In an explanatory context, the concept of seasons, for example, is related to the more general concept of orbital motion and the more specific concept of the Earth's axis' angle of inclination. This group did not directly investigate transfer of learning or problem solving.

Summary of Research on Learning and Teaching of Earth Science

Two difficulties face the instructor and the problem solver in Earth science. First, there is the problem of scale. As enormous as a thundercloud may seem, the frontal system of which it is a part can overwhelm the common scale of observation. Whether the topic is crustal history, stellar evolution, or paths of ocean currents, the scale of phenomena in Earth science presents an obstacle to solving problems.

Related to the problem of scale is the second difficulty in Earth science: the difficulty of visualization. Incomplete observation makes phenomena difficult to visualize, as does the fact that the phenomena of interest are usually complex systems. Maps, geometric models, computer models, and patterns can be used to help Earth scientists predict and explain events on the grandest scales of space, time, and energy.

Two other factors ease the difficulty of teaching Earth science. First, nearly all instruction in the field can tap a wealth of everyday experience and imagery. Second, knowledge of Earth science is pervasive: As students experience formal instruction in this science, they often can make unsuspected connections among their everyday experiences, often with relevance for understanding public policy issues such as hazardous waste disposal in karst terrain (limestone bedrock eroded by being dissolved in rain and groundwater to form caverns and sinkholes).

Abstract ideas must be brought down to Earth before students can master formal reasoning procedures. Research has made this abundantly clear. But other crucial aspects of problem solving in Earth science have yet to be investigated. Science educators have paid relatively little attention to the difficulties students experience in understanding the Earth sciences. We know too little about why some students succeed with problems requiring skill in visualization while others fail. Nor do we understand how some people come to grasp the scale of the phenomena of Earth science while others, failing to appreciate it, inhibit meaningful learning and problem solving.

There is no best way to teach or to measure student learning. Teachers should adapt their teaching to the kind of knowledge they expect to foster in their students. Rote learning style may sabotage efforts to teach problem solving if students become addicted to "right answer" science. Successful problem solvers seem to tolerate ambiguity, or at least multiple pathways of reasoning, in addition to knowing what they know, how to access information, and when to apply which parts. Often the role of the teacher is to make students uncomfortable with their present state of understanding, in order to initiate problem solving.

Recommendations for Teaching Problem Solving in the Earth Sciences

Some generalizations suggest themselves.
• Identify the conceptual models needed to reason in specific domains. For example, accounting for falling raindrops is not simple. How do droplets form in the sky? How do they get bigger? What keeps small droplets suspended? Do ice and water coexist in clouds? Do static charges make drops coalesce or not? When rain stops, why are there often still clouds in the sky? Good conceptual models have the raw materials for constructing answers to unusual questions as well as standard ones.
• Solve problems about phenomena familiar to students' experiences. Include

plenty of usable content that can resolve dilemmas, such as those dealing with condensation nuclei and the vapor pressure of ice crystals versus water droplets in the preceding example.

• Use props to assist visualization and abstract reasoning. If there are distortions of scale, make them explicit.

• Have students construct three-dimensional, two-dimensional, and verbal representations of problems. Link the levels of representation.

• Ask for oral and written restatements of problems, emphasizing precise meanings of terms and relationships in models.

• Connect abstractions to everyday experience by analogy: For example, compare escalators and merry-go-rounds to relative motion and orbit. Be certain that important relationships are well understood in the context of the analogies.

• Use imagination and imagery to express scale: Contrast ancient toeholds in the Betatakin ruins of the Anasazi people with the even-older excavation of the canyon and cavern. Try body language to convey patterns in Earth forms or motion in celestial bodies.

• Remember that the complexity of teaching and learning Earth science vastly exceeds the ability of research to offer prescriptive advice.

Earth science fascinates us because its problems take us well beyond our own experiences. At the same time, Earth science is the science of things beneath our feet, above our head, everywhere, always.

References

Ault, C. R., Jr. (1982, November). Time in geological explanations as perceived by elementary students. *Journal of Geological Education, 30*(5), 304–309.

Ault, C. R., Jr. (1985, September/October). Concept mapping as a text study strategy in Earth science. *Journal of College Science Teaching, 15*(1), 38–44.

Ault, C. R., Jr. (1986a). Expanded abstract of "Children's cosmographies: Understanding the Earth's shape and gravity" by C. Sneider and S. Pulos. [1983]. *Science Education, 67*(2), 205–222. Prepared for *Investigations in Science Education, 12*(1), 72–80.

Ault, C. R., Jr. (1986b, October). *Spatial vs. conceptual reasoning in the "first" structural geology lab.* Paper presented at meeting of the Association for the Education of Teachers of Science and the Society for College Science Teaching, North Central Regional Convention, Indianapolis.

Bloom, B. S. (Ed.). (1956). *Taxonomy of educational objectives. Handbook I: Cognitive domain.* New York: McKay.

Buchanan, B. G., and Shortlifte, E. H. (1984, 1985). *Rule-based expert systems: The MYCIN experiments of the Stanford Heuristic Programming Project.* Reading, MA: Addison-Wesley.

Champagne, A. B., and Klopfer, L. E. (1981, October). Structuring process skills and the solution of verbal problems involving science concepts. *Science Education, 65*(5), 493–511.

Champagne, A. B., Klopfer, L. E., Squires, D. A., and Desena, A. T. (1981, January). Structural representations of students' knowledge before and after science instruction. *Journal of Research in Science Teaching, 18*(1), 97–111.

Chiapetta, E. L., and Russell, J. M. (1982, January). The relationship among logical thinking, problem-solving instruction and knowledge and application of Earth science subject matter. *Science Education, 66*(1), 85–93.

Cohen, M. R. (1968). *The effect of small-scale geologic features on concepts of fluvial geology among fifth- and sixth-grade children.* Unpublished doctoral dissertation, Cornell University, Ithaca, NY.

Donaldson, M. (1982). Conservation: What is the question? In P. Bryant (Ed.), *Piaget: Issues and experiments* [Special issue]. *British Journal of Psychology, 73*(2), 99–200.

Finley, F. N. (1981, October). A philosophical approach to describing science content: An example from geologic classification. *Science Education, 65*(5), 513–519.

Finley, F. N. (1982, November). An empirical determination of concepts contributing to successful performance of a science process: A study of mineral classification. *Journal of Research in Science Teaching, 19*(8), 689–696.

Finley, F. N., and Smith, E. L. (1980a, July). Effects of strategy instruction on the learning, use, and vertical transfer of strategies. *Science Education, 64*(3), 367–375.

Finley, F. N., and Smith, E. L. (1980b, November). Student performance resulting from strategy-based instruction in a sequence of conceptually related tasks. *Journal of Research in Science Teaching, 17*(6), 583–593.

Happs, J. C. (1982a). *Glaciers: Science education research unit working paper no. 203.* Hamilton, New Zealand: University of Waikato. (ERIC Document Reproduction Service No. ED 236033)

Happs, J. C. (1982b). *Mountains: Science education research unit working paper no. 203.* Hamilton, New Zealand: University of Waikato. (ERIC Document Reproduction Service No. ED 236032)

Happs, J. C. (1982c). *Rocks and minerals: Science education research unit working paper no. 203.* Hamilton, New Zealand: University of Waikato. (ERIC Document Reproduction Service No. ED 236034)

Happs, J. C. (1982d). *Soils: Science education research unit working paper no. 203.* Hamilton, New Zealand: University of Waikato. (ERIC Document Reproduction Service No. ED 236031)

Janke, D. L., and Pella, M. O. (1972). Earth science concept list for grades K–12 curriculum contruction and evaluation. *Journal of Research in Science Teaching, 9*(3), 223–230.

Kelsey, L. J. G. (1980). The performance of college astronomy students on two of Piaget's projective infralogical grouping tasks and their relationship to problems dealing with phases of the moon. *Dissertation Abstracts International, 41*(6), 2539-A.

Kern, E. L., and Carpenter, J. R. (1984). Enhancement of student values, interests, and attitudes in Earth science through a field-oriented approach. *Journal of Geological Education, 32*(5), 299–305.

Klein, C. A. (1982). Children's concepts of the Earth and the Sun: A cross-cultural study. *Science Education, 65*(1), 95–107.

Mali, G., and Howe, A. (1979, October). Development of Earth and gravity concepts among Nepali children. *Science Education, 63*(5), 685–691.

Mayer, V. J., and Kozlow, M. J. (1980, September). Evaluation of a time series single-subject design used in an intensive study of concept understanding. *Journal of Research in Science Teaching, 17*(5), 445–461.

Monk, J. J., and Stallings, W. M. (1975, April). Classroom tests and achievement in problem solving in physical geography. *Journal of Research in Science Teaching, 12*(2), 133–138.

Monk, J. S. (1984). Using an intensive time series design to examine daily achievement and attitude of eighth- and ninth-grade Earth science students grouped by cognitive tendency, sex, and IQ. *Dissertation Abstracts International, 44*(9), 2727-A.

Novak, J. D. (1977). *A theory of education.* Ithaca, NY: Cornell University Press.

Novak, J. D. (1989). The role of content and process in the education of science teachers. In P. F. Brandwein and A. H. Passow (Eds.), *Gifted young in science: Potential through performance* (pp. 307–320). Washington, DC: NSTA.

Novak, J. D., and Gowin, D. B. (1984). *Learning how to learn.* Cambridge, MA: Cambridge University Press.

Novak, J. D., Gowin, D. B., and Johansen, G. T. (1983, October). The use of concept mapping and knowledge Vee mapping with junior high school science students. *Science Education, 67*(5), 625–645.

Nussbaum, J. (1979, June). Children's conceptions of Earth as a cosmic body: A cross-age study. *Science Education, 63*(1), 83–93.

Nussbaum, J., and Novak, J. D. (1976, October/December). Children's concepts of the Earth utilizing structured interviews. *Science Education, 60*(4), 535–550.

Osborne, R., and Freyberg, P. (1985). *Learning in science: The implications of children's science.* Portsmouth, NH: Heineman.

Rollins, M. M., Denton, J. J., and Janke, D. L. (1983, November/December). Attainment of selected Earth science concepts by Texas high school seniors. *Journal of Educational Research, 77*(2), 81–88.

Russell, J. M., and Chiapetta, E. L. (1981, July). The effects of a problem-solving strategy on the achievement of Earth science students. *Journal of Research in Science Teaching, 18*(4), 295–301.

Sneider, D., and Pulos, S. (1983, April). Children's cosmographies: Understanding the Earth's shape and gravity. *Science Education, 67*(2), 205–221.

Solarte, L. J. (1984). Analysis of Earth science topics for understanding levels of demand. *Dissertation Abstracts International, 44*(7), 2108-A.

Stepans, J., and Kuehn, C. (1985, September). What research says: Children's conceptions of weather. *Science and Children, 23*(1), 44–47.

Stevens, A. L., and Collins, A. (1980). Multiple conceptual models of a complex system. In R. E. Snow, P. A. Federico, and W. E. Montague (Eds.), *Aptitude learning and instruc-*

tion: *Cognitive process analyses of learning and problem solving* (Vol. 2). Hillsdale, NJ: Lawrence Erlbaum Associates.

Thomas, B. S. (1968). *An analysis of the effects of instructional methods upon selected outcomes of instruction in an interdisciplinary science unit.* Unpublished doctoral dissertation, University of Iowa, Iowa City.

Ulerick, S. L. (1982). The integration of knowledge from instructional discourses in a college-level geology course. *Dissertation Abstracts International, 42*(11), 4783-A.

Westerback, M. E., Gonzalez, C., and Primavera, L. H. (1984, December). Comparison of anxiety levels of students in introductory Earth science and geology courses. *Journal of Research in Science Teaching, 21*(9), 913-929.

Wiley, D. A. (1984). A comparison of the effectiveness of geological conceptual development within two field trip types as compared with classroom instruction. *Dissertation Abstracts International, 45*(1), 143-A.

Using Problem Solving in Physics Classes to Help Overcome Naive Misconceptions

Ray M. Snider
The College at New Paltz
State University of New York

Problem solving in science education has been the focus of much attention and concern in recent years. While secondary school and college science teachers and science educators historically have valued inquiry in science teaching, the study and promotion of problem-solving ability in science teaching has emerged recently as a high-priority area of activity.

A number of formal documents at both state and local levels affirm this. For instance, an NSTA position statement (1982/1985/1989) underscored the need for cultivating problem-solving ability in high school. In noting that current problems can be solved only "... by persons educated in the ideas and processes of science and technology... ," the statement cites scientific literacy as "...basic for living, working, and decision making in the 1980s and beyond" (p. 162).

The NSTA statement recommends that "high school level laboratory and field activities should emphasize not only the acquisition of knowledge but also problem solving and decision making" (p. 164). Earlier, the New York Regents (1980) reached a similar decision, citing the development of skills in problem defining and solving as one of the state's specific goals for elementary and secondary education. The Regents saw these skills as necessary for lifetime learning, enabling appropriate response to the world's changing demands, opportunities, and values.

Problem Solving: Some Definitions

Although "problem solving" in physics education is perceived and used in various ways, there is some agreement that it encourages inquiry and activities in which unknowns are sought.

D. R. Woods (1980, June) defines problem solving in physics as an activity by which the best value for an unknown is obtained, subject to a set of conditions and constraints. He deals with prerequisites brought to the problem-solving situation (knowledge, experience, learning skills, motivation, communication, and group skills); various strategies for problem solving (e.g., define, think, plan, act, look back); hints, elements (including analysis and creativity), and types (involving degree of difficulty, information given, and types of unknowns). On the basis of his research, Woods concludes that problem solving is an identifiable, teachable skill, a discipline with a structure that we are just beginning to perceive.

J. Kilpatrick (1982), confining his approach to problems which could be "posed or solved" in school mathematics classes, advances the notion that problem solving is associated with a situation in which a goal is attainable but a direct route to it is blocked. Problem solving is then involved in the process undertaken to reach the goal. Kilpatrick analyzes problem solving through mathematical, pedagogical, psychological, and sociological perspectives. Since many believe that there is an intimate connection between physics and mathematics, his analysis might prove useful for problem solving in physics classrooms and laboratories.

In this framework, approaches to high school and college general physics could be addressed by methods of problem solving as well as in the light of the knowledge generated by problem-solving efforts. Problems pursued by Archimedes, Boyle, Newton, Faraday, Kirchhoff, Planck, Bohr, Einstein, and others—the basis of physics—would form the content of physics courses, content that would be seen as evolving from consideration of problem-solving processes.

Kilpatrick's pedagogical perspective relates to the kinds of strategies or approaches taken in solving problems in physics. The various roles he sees for problem solving in mathematics—such as introducing a topic, providing motivation, reinforcing techniques, and synthesizing what has been learned—are equally appropriate for physics.

G. Polya (1981) also classifies problems from a pedagogical perspective. He defines several approaches:

- One rule right under your nose—The problem is to be solved by mechanical application of a rule just presented or discussed.
- Application with some choice—[The problem is to be] solved by applying a rule given earlier in class; [this] involves some judgment on the part of the student.
- Choice of a combination—The student is required to combine two or more rules given in class. . . .
- Approaching research level—[The] problem's solution requires a novel combination of rules and has many ramifications requiring a high level of independent thought and plausible reasoning. (vol. 2, p. 139)

R. G. Fuller, R. Karplus, and A. E. Lawson (1977, February) offer a useful summary and discussion of J. Piaget's work on reasoning and problem solving. (Cf. Inhelder and Piaget, 1958.) Piaget's theory of the development of reasoning describes progress from an initial sensory-motor stage through three other successive stages—reasoning on preoperational, concrete, and formal levels. Because high school physics students are generally at the formal reasoning stage, most of them can

use hypotheses and deduction in their reasoning. They can accept an unproven hypothesis, deduce its consequences in the light of other known information, and then verify empirically whether, in fact, those consequences occur. Furthermore, they can reflect upon their own reasoning to look for inconsistencies. They can check their own results in numerical calculations against order-of-magnitude estimates. (Fuller, et al p. 26)

According to the summary offered by Fuller and his colleagues,

> The Piaget hypothesis is that a challenging but solvable problem will place persons into an initial state of disequilibrium. Then, through their own efforts at bringing together this challenge with their past experiences and what they learn from teachers and peers, they will gradually reorganize their thinking and solve the problem successfully. This success will establish a new and more stable equilibrium with increased understanding of the subject matter and increased problem-solving capability, that is, intellectual development. (p. 28)

In contrast to Piaget's attention to "disequilibrium," D. P. Butts' (1964) focus is on the following elements as important orderly aspects of problem-solving behavior:

1. Early formation of a hypothesis
2. Specific experiments with related variables as contrasted with random guessing
3. Introduction of a control to test the validity of a hypothesis tested
4. Specific attempts at verification of the hypothesis. (p. 117)

Another seminal thinker on problem solving is B. S. Bloom. J. M. Russell and G. L. Chiappetta (1981) compare Bloom's view of problem solving with that of R. M. Gagne (1970). Gagne sees problem solving as the highest form of learning—more complex forms of learning depend upon processes previously acquired in simpler forms and then recalled and applied in a novel manner. The new higher-order rule is a learned response, which is generalizable and transferable to a class of related problems. In contrast, Bloom's model of problem solving calls for application of different levels of thinking. Here, students select abstractions from learned repertoires and use them to solve problems.

A. B. Champagne and L. E. Klopfer (1981) express concern that many students are deficient in the higher order mental skills, which are essential components of reflective thinking and problem solving. Regarding a definition of problem solving, Champagne and Klopfer report that ". . . despite extensive efforts on the part of science educators, there is no clear, complete definition of the meaning of problem solving in the context of science education. And yet, such a definition is prerequisite to implementing problem-solving instruction in science classrooms" (p. 5). They cite a need for carefully developed observational studies of the behavior of good problem solvers in action.

How is Problem Solving Currently Taught in Physics?

Physics instruction in high school and college general physics classes is usually geared to promoting a firm grasp of concepts. This is appropriate. But problem solving is by and large limited to applying formulas to sets of exercises at the end of textbook chapters (Larkin, 1979; Reif, 1977; Clement, 1977, 1978a, 1978b, 1979). Answering these questions is sometimes perceived as the main criterion for indicating understanding of the subject matter of the problem. But such exercises are not really problem solving—they are oversimplified into what P. F. Brandwein (1962) called "actually . . . steps in problem doing—since the solution is already known" (p. 10). In the usual situation, the student is expected to consider a law or equation recently presented and discussed and to use numerical values given for all but one of the variables to determine the value of the remaining variable. This type of exercise is typically supplemented by laboratory exercises which verify principles or laws of physics. While this procedure may promote concept development, it is inappropriate and inadequate for developing problem-solving abilities. Students need the opportunity to engage in academically productive problem solving.

Researchers in the 1960s and early 1970s examined teacher-student verbal interaction in elementary and secondary school science classrooms and laboratories. For example, a one-year study of 17 high school physics classes in upstate New York produced normative data on verbal communication in physics classrooms and laboratories (Snider, 1966). Communication in the physics lab was compared with that in classrooms when other major activities were underway, such as lectures, teacher demonstrations, or recitation and discussion. Results showed that, when teachers spoke in the laboratory, they gave greater percentages of one-way information, directions, and criticism than in any of the major classroom activities. There was also relatively less praise, acceptance of student ideas, and questioning during labs than during the classroom activities. This authoritarian quality is the opposite of what one would expect if laboratory time is focused on problem solving. It is consistent, however, with the verification type of laboratory activity that prevailed at that time and that, reports indicate, continues in high school and college general physics laboratories.

L. S. Shulman and P. Tamir (1973) include a comprehensive review of the classroom observational studies in their analysis of research on science teaching. They report, "The inevitable conclusion of such studies is that inquiry is preached far more widely than practiced" (p. 1135). This still seems to be the case.

A long history of declining interest and enrollment in high school physics is part of a crisis in physics education. J. W. Layman's comprehensive 1983 assessment cites a 1982 analysis by the American Institute of Physics, Manpower Statistics Division, using data from the National Center for Education Statistics, which showed that only 20 percent of graduating high school seniors had taken a physics course. If 60 percent of the students who start high school graduate, then about 12 percent of the nation's youth take a physics course during their schooling. This is cause for concern in view of the importance of physics as a basic science and the ever-increasing need for scientific literacy, including problem solving, in contemporary technological society.

There is good news as well. J. M. Wilson and T. C. Ingoldsby (1983, September) identified and described a number of exemplary physics programs, summarizing,

> Excellence in physics teaching is not confined by region or type of community and can be found in large cities, small towns, or rural farming communities.
>
> Although the variations from program to program are great, there are a number of common ingredients found in all. Enthusiasm, visibility, recruiting, fun, excitement, laboratory experiences, computers, a supportive community, local scientific interactions, and an interest in the breadth of the science and mathematics experience appear to make up a recipe for outstanding programs, but the key element is an understanding teacher or teachers. (p. 52)

Other elements Wilson and Ingoldsby found to foster problem-solving ability are mandatory comprehensive research projects; requirements that students take at least one course each in biology, chemistry, and physics before taking a second year of any science; hands-on use of computers; required participation in competitions; laboratory emphasis on investigative activities; and an extensive curriculum with many physics offerings at various levels.

Many high schools promote opportunities for some students to engage in research or research-related enrichment programs. The Westinghouse Science Talent Search and the New York State Science Congress (sponsored by the Science Teachers Association of New York State) are examples of efforts focused on inquiry, i.e., on problem solving. Unfortunately, relatively few students participate in programs such as these. The Physics Olympics and Science Olympiad, programs in which teams of students attempt to solve problems in competition sessions, are expanding in terms of interest and participation.

Woods (1983) inquired about the presence and nature of problem-solving instruction at colleges and universities in the United States, Canada, and England, collecting responses from 80 institutions. Ninety-two percent of the respondents indicated some efforts to promote problem-solving activities. Twenty-nine percent reported at least one special course in problem solving. Of these, about 16 percent offered the course through an engineering department; 4 percent had a separate physics course on problem solving; 4 percent offered a course in another discipline. Problem-solving instruction is most commonly part of other courses (in 51 percent of the institutions); in about half of these cases it is offered through engineering courses and in a tenth, through physics courses.

Occasional innovations and/or special efforts at teaching problem solving include using audio tape cassettes on which solutions are discussed in detail (Chagnon, 1980).

How Should Problem Solving Be Taught in Physics?

An Approach From Mathematics. Problem solving in mathematics has relevance for problem solving in physics. According to Kilpatrick, research in the late 1970s and early 1980s shows that expert problem solvers in mathematics have the following general skills and attributes:
- prerequisite knowledge
- organized approaches or strategies
- ability to create, analyze, simplify, and generalize
- awareness of heuristics appropriate to their preferred style of solving problems

Researchers in mathematics education conclude that students need appropriate knowledge of subject matter, specific techniques for doing mathematics, and general thinking skills. Most mathematics educators support the need for practice with specific attention to various techniques and approaches. The same general approach might apply to teaching and learning physics, particularly in reference to developing problem-solving abilities.

Kilpatrick argues that mathematics instruction should also prepare students to succeed in solving other problems. Of mathematics instruction, he writes "problems are usually presented to students as tasks to be done rather than as opportunities to learn, and pressures to perform rapidly and efficiently often subvert a teacher's encouragement of a reflective approach and an openness to alternative ideas in attacking problems" (p. 4).

His statement also applies to some physics instruction. A consensus among writers about math and physics emphasizes four roles problem solving could play in the teaching of physics. Problem solving could offer a
- means to motivate students by introducing a topic
- source of exercise material for practicing skills
- way of synthesizing what students have learned
- vehicle for developing a sense of the subject overall

More Participation. A key point throughout the literature is that students must have opportunities to experiment or explore in the laboratory and to participate in designing some of the experiments. This element is conspicuously absent in most schools. Laboratory programs should not be limited to directed activity to verify textbook concepts or laws.

Teachers could tell students, for example, what a pendulum is and define the term *period*. Students could then face the task of exploring possible relationships between the period and other characteristics, such as the mass of the suspended bob, the length of the pendulum, and the angle of maximum displacement from the vertical. Evaluation would hinge on decisions made in developing the experiment and in generating and interpreting data. Teachers could encourage students to employ various techniques in analyzing data, such as plotting graphs with combinations of variables to various powers (exponents) to discover some combination that would suggest a straight line graph. This graph would be the basis for discerning an equation connecting the variables.

The student might eventually discover that the square of the period versus the length would lead to a straight line graph. In dealing with the generated equation, $T^2 = k_1 L + k_2$ (where the ks are constants), the student would take (at least numerically), steps to evaluate the constants from the graph taking whatever time is necessary (within reason). The problem need not be solved in one laboratory period. The point is that the textbook formula for the period of a simple pendulum is probably far less important for the student than the experience of designing and conducting an experiment to discover a relationship and to solve a problem.

Numerous problems of this sort can be readily contrived in all areas of physics. Consider, for example, distance of free fall from rest and the time of free fall; or, for a particular mass m constrained to a circular path of a particular radius r, the centripetal force and the speed along the path. Different students could be investigating different problems: All the students don't have to do the same laboratory activity at the same time.

Dimensional Analysis. Dimensional analysis—that is, examination of the units of physical entities such as force, velocity, and momentum—offers promise as a technique to assist problem solving. In a study involving two high school classes studying kinematics and dynamics, E. R. Kirkland (1981) offered the experimental group a special emphasis on dimensional analysis. Later testing showed this group of students significantly to outperform the controls in solving problems involving kinematics and dynamics. Although limited by its small sample of students and brief duration, the Kirkland study's support of dimensional analysis as a teachable problem-solving tool is worth noting.

Several Approaches. Promoting good organization and written and oral communication skills would enhance problem solving. R. F. Gunstone and R. T. White (1981) have experimented by raising questions about some physical phenomenon and asking students to predict what will happen. After a demonstration, students are asked to resolve discrepancies between their predictions and what actually happened.

A. Bork and J. Lochhead (1980) suggest that, after checking students' work to see if the solutions were reasonable, teachers should ask students to solve problems using two or more methods. P. Landry and R. Moore (1980) agree. They suggest that physics teachers include in each week's assignment an exercise in which a phenomenon is demonstrated and measurements are made, with the problem posed based on those measurements. Landry and Moore also offer students problems containing extraneous numerical information and encourage them to learn to check their answers by means of alternative solutions.

A number of things can keep students from solving problems effectively. Among them are what M. Scheerer (1983, April) calls "fixations," where the student "... clings misguidedly to a false premise or assumption regarding the problem to be solved." Examples of mistaken fixations are summarized frequently in much of the research on problem solving in physics classrooms and laboratories—for example, many students think that the velocity of an object in free fall depends upon its mass (Champagne, Klopfer, and Gunstone, 1981) or that two objects on parallel tracks have the same speed at any point at which they have the same position (Trowbridge and McDermott, 1980, December).

Naive Misconceptions

Students' naive misconceptions can get in the way of their problem solving in physics; teachers must deal carefully with the beliefs their students bring with them to physics classes. D. K. Jira, M. McCloskey, and B. F. Green (1981) suggest that educators should not act as if students simply lack correct information. Substantial research indicates that students begin the study of physics with strong systems of beliefs about various topics, systems which seem logical and reasonable and are resistant to change. Jira and her colleagues list common misconceptions that affect students' problem-solving performance in physics. These convictions cause particular problems in connection with force, gravity, velocity versus acceleration, and Newton's first law. For example, as the research of Jira and her colleagues indicates, many physics students think a force is required to keep a body in motion, and many maintain their belief in this so-called "impetus theory," which seems logical in terms of everyday experience. Teachers aware of the pervasiveness of this misconception could make adjustments in their teaching to take it into account and thus enhance students' problem solving. Jira and her colleagues posit that students' integrated systems of beliefs about the behavior of objects in motion can hinder efforts at problem solving. These "naive beliefs," which are quite resistant to modification, were evident among students who had studied physics as well those who had not. Students often incorporated sophisticated terminology into expressions of their naive beliefs.

Champagne and Klopfer (1981) also call on teachers to recognize and account for preinstruction conceptualizations when they design instruction. They advise teachers to modify these ideas slowly, one by one, rather than trying to replace them all at once with valid formal structures. Champagne, Klopfer, and Gunstone (1981) stress the idea that ". . . students' comprehension of science instruction may be influenced more by their world knowledge than by the intended meaning of either their teachers or the authors of textbooks they read" (p. 12). For example, many students, often claiming empirical support, think free-fall velocity depends on mass.

Research at the University of Massachusetts in the Cognitive Development Project has led J. Clement (1981) to suggest the presence of "inherently difficult conceptual primitives" in physics. Such "primitives," prerequisites for a grasp of higher order concepts, cover two broad areas: fundamental quantities, such as mass, acceleration, momentum, charge, energy, and the like; and unifying principles, such as Newton's laws, conservation laws, the atomic model, and others. According to Clement, an infirm grasp of these concepts affects students' ability to solve problems involving motion. In analyzing students' understanding of the relationship between force and motion, Clement confirmed the observation of Jira and her colleagues that many students assume a continuing force behind every motion and that science courses do not necessarily correct this notion. In one experimental situation, 31 of 43 engineering students who had completed a mechanics course still shared this misconception. Based on this kind of evidence, Clement expresses concern that students' superficial knowledge of formulas and how to manipulate them in solving numerical physics problems can mask inadequate qualitative understanding of key concepts and laws. He concludes that

> it may be necessary to devote more attention in physics courses to conceptual primitives at the qualitative level than is currently practiced, and we suspect that teaching strategies limited to expository presentation may be unlikely to succeed in this area. The "motion implies a force" preconception is not likely to disappear simply because students have been exposed to the standard view in courses. Attempts to "cover" a very large syllabus and to present physics in a formal mathematical language may preclude students from learning basic qualitative concepts that give them an intuitive understanding of the subject. (p. 4)

Research by Gunstone and White (1981), using as subjects 467 Australian college students with two years of high school physics, also supports the view of Clement, Champagne and Klopfer, and Jira and her colleagues that many students retain their preinstructional views of phenomena in spite of physics course work. In short, misconceptions or "alternative knowledge structures," which surface in much of the research on problem solving, often seem to govern what students believe, no matter what they're taught.

M. C. Linn (1981, April) has also explored the influence of student expectations on reasoning performance, concluding that there is a connection between the variables adolescents expect to govern an observed outcome in the laboratory and their reasoning performance. For example, students engaged in predicting displaced volume using submerged metal cubes of different densities frequently associated the volume of displaced water with the weight of the submerged cube. They intuitively selected weight as the significant variable, and they were reluctant to consider any others. According to Linn, the students were aware of the "logical strategy for controlling variables ... but [could] apply it only to their expected variables. Therefore, subjects [in this case, students] might appear to lack a [problem-solving] strategy, when actually their failure is due to inaccurate expectations" (p. 7).

In research on student performance in an introductory college physics course, Champagne, Klopfer, and J. H. Anderson (1980, December) investigated the combined effect of preconceptions about motion and of skills in mathematics and reasoning upon mastering classical mechanics. To measure success, they used a composite score based on two hour-long examinations and the mechanics items from the final examination given at the end of the course.

A comparison of the protocols of the 17 highest-scoring students showed that these students used the technical terms and concepts of mechanics and were aware of having accepted the Newtonian paradigm. Analysis indicated that

> each student usually has a rich accumulation of interrelated ideas that constitute a personal system of common-sense beliefs about motion. These common-sense intuitive ideas, based on years of experience with moving objects, serve the students satisfactorily in describing the world. Nevertheless, this belief system is quite different from the formal system of Newtonian mechanics that the physics course seeks to teach. It seems useful to view the students' preinstructional belief system and the course's target of mechanics as competing paradigms. (p. 1078)

Champagne and her colleagues believe that students must undergo a reconceptualization, a paradigm shift, in order to learn mechanics successfully. Characterizing students' beliefs as "fundamentally Aristotelian," they reported that students thought that objects fall at constant speed and that the speed depends on the weight or the mass of the object. However, students who knew that objects freely falling in the laboratory do, indeed, accelerate, proposed that the acceleration resulted from an increase in the force of gravity as the body approached the ground. Hoping to promote a "scientific revolution" in students' conceptualizing, Champagne and her colleagues wrote,

> It is not enough for instructors to present classical mechanics as a collection of facts, or even to present classical mechanics in a structured way....The challenge for physics instructors is to enable the students to discover for themselves the limitations and inadequacies of an Aristotelian framework as well as the far-reaching explanatory powers of the Newtonian paradigm. (p. 1078)

In a follow-up study, Champagne, Klopfer, and Gunstone (1981) had junior high school and beginning college physics students compare the times for two objects of equal size and shape, but different mass, to fall equal distances from rest. Basing their explanations in misinformation about Galileo's experiment with falling cannon balls of different weights, a significant number of students at both levels predicted that the heavier object would fall faster. According to the authors, students "remember the part of Galileo's experiment that is consistent with their prediction and forget the part of the experiment that is inconsistent with their prediction" (p. 13).

D. E. Trowbridge and L. C. McDermott have conducted extensive studies of beginning college physics students' thinking in situations involving motion at constant velocity (1980, December) and uniformly accelerated motion (1981, March). They found that such students associated position with speed when observing the motion of steel balls rolling at constant speed in straight channels (U-shaped in cross section). In a "two-pass" situation (described in 1980, December), ball (1),* launched at a greater initial speed and later than another (2), constantly decelerated as it rolled up a steady incline. First, ball 1 passed ball 2, which was travelling at a constant speed. But then 2 passed 1. Asked if there were any instances at which the speeds of the two balls were the same, some students realized that since ball 1, with its declining speed, started out faster than steady-speed ball 2 and wound up slower, there had to be at least one point when the two balls had the same speed. However, many concluded that there were *two* points in time when the balls had the same speed—namely (they thought), the two instances in which one ball passed the other. These students were convinced that the two balls had the same speed at the points in time when they were at the same position. Actually, only once did the balls have the same speed, and that was not when they had the same position.

Superimposed plots of position versus time made this fact evident. The graph for ball 1 (initially faster but decelerating) is a curve, while the constant-speed ball 2 produces a straight line. At two points on the graph, the balls have the same position, but at only one point is the slope of a tangent line to the curve the same as the slope of the straight-line graph of ball 2. At this point in time only, the decelerating ball has the same speed as the steady-speed ball. Nevertheless, students insisted that there had to be *two* points in time at which the balls had the same speed, because there were two instances when they were next to each other, that is, adjacent on tracks going in the same horizontal direction.

Like many others, this misconception was hard to dislodge, and it persisted in spite of instruction. Trowbridge and McDermott discussed the analysis emerging from student interviews:

> Students lack an adequate procedure for deciding if two objects have the same instantaneous speed. Indeed, they focus attention on the perceptually obvious phenomenon of passing to make the required comparison. A successful comparison usually required that an individual focus attention on the separation between the balls and verify an instant when this separation is neither increasing nor decreasing. (p. 1023)

Trowbridge and McDermott executed a second speed comparison but without passing. In this design, one ball starts with high velocity, decelerates, and then comes to rest. The other ball starts from rest at a point ahead of the first ball and accelerates uniformly by rolling down an inclined U channel. The first never overtakes the second.

There is a point in time when both balls have the same speed. If students were using a position criterion to determine whether or not the speeds were the same, they would decide "No" because the balls don't pass each other. And, indeed, this is what happened. Trowbridge and McDermott report that in this case, they saw

> a student associating the idea of being ahead with having a greater speed. The use of relative position for comparing speeds was as common on the second speed comparison as on the first.
>
> As in the case of the first speed comparison task, logical arguments did not necessarily influence student responses. Even after satisfactorily describing the speed of [one] ball ... as decreasing to zero and the [other] ... as increasing from zero, some students observing the demonstration would still claim that the speeds were never the same since the balls never passed each other. (p. 1024)

---

*The balls have been numbered for convenience in summarizing the research.

Trowbridge and McDermott varied instruction on kinematics with different types of groups. They concluded that

> For some students the acquisition of physical concepts seems to depend strongly upon the establishment of satisfactory connections between these new concepts and protoconcepts with which the student is already familiar. In fact, among the academically disadvantaged students such connections seemed to be crucial in order for new concepts to take on meaning. Thus, a conscious effort should be made to try to help students relate physical concepts to their experience, especially if they are to be expected to satisfy the criterion for understanding used in this investigation: the successful application of concepts to real situations. (p. 1028)

Trowbridge and McDermott's follow-up study (1981, March), involving uniformly accelerated motion with the ball and U-channel type apparatus, led to similar conclusions. Students compared accelerations in terms of positions, thinking that the same position implied the same acceleration. Sixty percent of students in precourse interviews confused concepts of velocity and acceleration. Overall, only about 20 percent of students (in a variety of groups) in precourse interviews used ratios to compare accelerations; 80 percent frequently did not understand the concept of acceleration as a ratio of change in velocity to corresponding change in time.

In a study of engineering students' conceptions about simple circuits, N. Fredette and Lochhead (1980) asked students—given three wires, a bulb, and a standard flashlight battery—to light the bulb. The researchers concluded that "many students enter college-level introductory physics courses without a clear understanding . . . [of the] passing-through process. We believe that the conception must be dealt with explicitly" (p. 198). Students did not understand either the concept that a circuit element has an "in" and an "out" in direct current circuits or that there is such a thing as a complete circuit.

Some Attempts at Remediation: Some Failures, Some Suggestions

Perhaps heuristics could help overcome naive misconceptions. In a study of problem solving in high school physics, D. S. True (1975) compared the performance of a group of 46 students instructed in Polya's heuristics (1957, 1981) to another group of 42 taught Daniels' method of scanning the properties of the components or variables in a problem. A control group received instruction in problem solving without heuristics.

While a large majority of the students were able to do the mathematics and recognize the physics concepts, members of the control group were unsuccessful with the problem-solving physics test administered at the end of the semester. True reported that "a lack of mathematical skill is not more or less responsible for the students' failure to solve the problems correctly than is the lack of knowledge regarding physical concepts" (p. 6532A). The major cause of students' difficulty in problem solving was their inability to understand the problem and to apply the concepts. The two experimental groups, which were exposed to problem-solving heuristics, did significantly better than the control group on the problem-solving test.

Another researcher investigated the efficacy of expository aids and drills in banishing certain misconceptions. R. W. Hohly (1980) developed and tested a model of six skills through which college students solve complex physics problems in a calculus-based introductory physics course. Hohly believes that problem solving allows students to "derive suitable equations from underlying principles on examination questions" (p. 188A). However, the students did not adequately develop their ability to recognize which laws apply and to associate definitions with laws, making Hohly conclude that developing these skills through problem-solving activity in the course is not feasible. He therefore calls for developing expository materials to teach law recognition and for drills to teach the definitions.

Some Conclusions: Toward More Successful Problem Solving in Physics

One Approach: Extra Help. In a recent experiment with ninth-grade physics classes in Israel, J. Idar and U. Ganiel (1985) developed, implemented, and evaluated a program of remedial instruction. Through an analysis of abilities students need to perform in the course, Idar and Ganiel identified four major ability domains—reading comprehension, analyzing experimental results, doing algebra, and making graphs. Because these domains were viewed as prerequisites for the course, students were tested to identify deficiencies. A composite of the four tests provided a "background" measure. Idar and Ganiel also developed an investigative laboratory questionnaire (an adaptation of the clinical interview Piaget developed) to obtain insight into other difficulties students encountered in the course. Students and teachers were individually interviewed as well. Results showed that the majority of students entered the physics course without the necessary prerequisites.

Idar and Ganiel perceived a "feedback gap" in physics classrooms resulting from a lack of adequate diagnoses. They report:

> Typical classroom assessment procedures, with their traditional focus on the production of "correct" answers, seemed inadequate for discovering what students really thought and how they really interpreted what they were taught.
>
> This lack of accurate diagnostic information apparently had a negative impact on the functioning of both teachers and students. (p. 129)

Experimental-group teachers in classrooms and laboratories developed a remedial teaching method. For 10 to 20 minutes, immediately following exposure to selected concepts and experiences, students were required to respond to written questions intended to assess their perceptions and understandings and to expose common misconceptions and miscomprehensions. Immediately after responding to the questions, all students received written feedback, which provided correct answers and explanations. This process was remedial for students who lacked appropriate understanding; in addition, it provided general reinforcement for those who answered the questions correctly. Idar and Ganiel believe their method, which consumes little classroom time and demands minimal paperwork, is feasible for typical classrooms, and they write:

> the results obtained indicate that the use of these manuals and teaching procedures brought about a substantial improvement in achievement. After seven months of implementation in schools all over the country in the natural settings of mixed . . . ability ninth-grade students, the mean achievement score of the experimental group was higher than the control group by approximately 5 standard error units. (p. 137)

In their concluding remarks, Idar and Ganiel echo others' views and provide some encouragement:

> A major complication apparently encountered in teaching physics to average and low-ability students, in natural classroom settings, is that these students tend to interpret their class and laboratory experiences in ways that frequently differ from and contradict the purpose of these activities. Misconceptions brought by the student, or created during the learning process in class, are often tenaciously held and are difficult to alter through conventional teaching means. These misconceptions are also difficult to detect. Many examination, classroom, and home-

work . . . questions can . . . be answered by recalling verbal knowledge or by applying formula-manipulation techniques.

The results of this study indicate that it is possible to address misconceptions directly, in natural classroom settings and to solve [some] of them. (p. 138)

Another Approach From Piaget's Theories. Other recent efforts focus on learning theory stemming from Piaget but apply to secondary school and college general physics instruction. J. W. Renner, M. R. Abraham, and H. H. Birnie (1986) have investigated the "functioning factor" of Piaget's model. "Functioning" consists of "assimilation," "disequilibrium," "accommodation," and "organization." The purpose of Renner and his colleagues was to see if these processes actually occur as students learn physics. The authors describe phases of learning, including an exploration phase, in which students interact with equipment and materials, leading to a phase in which they deal with generated data. This phase leads to "concept invention," followed by "concept development" in a "discovery" phase, which leads to "concept implementation." Here, the student uses new thoughts to explain other phenomena. After 65 individual student interviews in connection with 7 laboratory experiences, Renner and his colleagues concluded that the efficacy of the Piagetian assimilation/accommodation learning model was supported.

To "probe and extend Piaget's theory" (p. 841), E. Poduska and D. G. Phillips (1986) investigated 100 college students' conceptions of speed. They explored Piagetian tasks (conservation of distance; asymmetric series of speeds; one-to-many circular speeds; symmetric speeds; time and proportional reasoning). Poduska and Phillips also investigated the processes students use in thinking about speed. One noteworthy aspect of the study is its extension of a test of Piaget's theory to college students. Poduska and Phillips found a particular sequence of development for thinking about speed phenomena, writing that "the tasks scaled according to [Piaget's] theory, even though some of the subjects had a physics background and others did not" (p. 846).

Lawson (1985) provided a comprehensive review of research on formal reasoning and Piaget's theory of formal thought. Studies reviewed address one or more of the following questions:

- What role does biological maturation play in the development of formal reasoning?
- Are Piaget's formal tasks reliable and valid?
- Does formal reasoning constitute a unified general mode of intellectual functioning?
- How does the presence or absence of formal reasoning affect school achievement?
- Can formal reasoning be taught?
- What is the structural or functional nature of advanced reasoning?

Lawson believes that Piaget has provided the schools with an important framework for understanding and developing reasoning abilities, even though there remain some unresolved questions about Piagetian theory.

Help From Hindsight. In another effort, Woods (1980) gives specific suggestions for problem solving, including putting the emphasis on learning how a problem *should have been* solved after it *has been* solved. Woods believes this approach helps learners to translate words to symbols and/or diagrams. He feels teachers should promote students' ability to organize "chunks" of information into larger "chunks" to develop overall structures. Teachers should help students to discover the structure in the physics content taught. Woods reports that all aspects of problem-solving skills examined show interdependence with learning skills, noting that this symbiosis is especially true of creative problem solving. He concludes that many of the ideas about problem solving can be synthesized and major headway can be made in teaching its concepts.

Questions for Success. Wilson and Ingoldsby (1983) also discuss conditions for excellence. "Yes" answers to the following questions, developed by an American Association of Physics Teachers committee chaired by Willa Ramsey, would strongly suggest "Places Where Things are Right" in the study of physics:

- Do students with different interests and backgrounds pursue, enjoy, and profit from the study of physics?
- Do students understand the relation of physical principles . . . to their personal experiences?
- Are students able to complete and explain the results of guided experiences related to their physical environment?
- Are students able to distinguish between observation and inference, opinion and fact?
- Are students able to recognize the important physical principles underlying a given issue?
- Can students gather, record, organize, and explain the implications of data?
- Do students understand the nature of scientific "theory," its value and implications?
- [Are students] encouraged to build a structure of ideas and concepts within the physics course that will help [them] evaluate the problems of the real world?
- Does the course involve qualitative and quantitative analyses based on estimates, thereby approximating real world situations?
- Do students develop skills necessary for continuing growth and knowledge of science throughout life?
- Does the physics program fit within the goals, objectives, and philosophy of the total school? (p. 53)

Wilson and Ingoldsby add that a significant fraction of the student population should be reached by the physics program. (p. 53)

In Sum. This accumulation of research makes clear that experimentation with the learning and teaching of physics yields valuable insights about both processes, insights that can ultimately advance teachers' ability to cultivate problem-solving abilities. Contemporary learning theory and research on physics teaching can offer teachers a great deal; therefore, opportunity, support, and encouragement should be substantially expanded for research on teaching.

Relatively little of this kind of study of teaching and learning, however, is occurring in high school and college physics classrooms and laboratories. Physics teachers need to get involved with studying problem solving at whatever level of complexity is feasible and appropriate. Supported by proper allocations of time and resources, researchers should share efforts, ideas, and findings with their colleagues. Such investigative efforts cannot fail to have a positive impact on physics instruction in general and on the promotion of problem-solving ability in particular.

References

Bork, A., and Lochhead, J. (1980). Teaching problem solving with computers. *Problem Solving, 1*(12), 7.

Brandwein, P. F. (1962). *Elements in a strategy for teaching science in the elementary school* (The Burton Lecture). Cambridge, MA: Harvard University Press.

Butts, D. P. (1964). The evolution of problem solving in science. *Journal of Research in Science Teaching, 2*(2), 116–122.

Chagnon, P. (1980, June). *Problem solutions on audiotape cassettes.* Paper presented at the meeting of the American Association of Physics Teachers, Troy, NY.

Champagne, A. B., and Klopfer, L. E. (1981). Problem solving as outcome and method in science teaching: Insights from sixty years of experience. *School Science and Mathematics, 81*(1), 3-8.

Champagne, A. B., Klopfer, L. E., and Anderson, J. H. (1980, December). Factors influencing the learning of classical mechanics. *American Journal of Physics, 48*(12), 1074-1079.

Champagne, A. B., Klopfer, L. E., and Gunstone, R. F. (1981). Student beliefs about gravity and motion. *Problem Solving, 2*(12), 12-14.

Clement, J. (1977). *Some types of knowledge used in understanding physics* (Tech. Rep.). Amherst, MA: University of Massachusetts.

Clement, J. (1978a). *Formula-centered knowledge versus conceptual understanding in physics* (Tech. Rep.). Amherst, MA: University of Massachusetts, Department of Physics and Astronomy, Cognitive Development Project.

Clement, J. (1978b). *Cataloguing students' conceptual models in physics* (Final report to the National Science Foundation/RULE [Research in Undergraduate Learning Experience] Program). Amherst, MA: University of Massachusetts, Department of Physics and Astronomy.

Clement, J. (1979). *Limitations of formula-centered approaches in problem solving in physics and engineering* (Tech. Rep.). Amherst, MA: University of Massachusetts, Department of Physics and Astronomy, Cognitive Development Project.

Clement, J. (1981). *Students' preconceptions in physics and Galileo's discussion of falling bodies* (Tech. Rep.). Amherst, MA: University of Massachusetts, Department of Physics and Astronomy, Cognitive Development Project.

Fredette, N. and Lochhead, J. (1980, March). Student conceptions of simple circuits. *The Physics Teacher, 18*(3), 194-198.

Fuller, R. G., Karplus, R., and Lawson, A. E. (1977, February). Can physics develop reasoning? *Physics Today, 30*(2), 23-28.

Gagne, R. M. (1970). *The condition of learning.* New York: Holt.

Gunstone, R. F., and White, R. T. (1981). Understanding of gravity-related phenomena. *Problem Solving, 2*(12), 4-6.

Hohly, R. W. (1980). Development of basic problem-solving skills in calculus-based introductory physics. *Dissertation Abstracts International, 41*, 188A. (University Microfilms No. 8015260)

Idar, J., and Ganiel, U. (1985). Learning difficulties in high school physics: Development of a remedial teaching method and assessment of its impact on achievement. *Journal of Research in Science Teaching, 22*(2), 127-140.

Inhelder, B., and Piaget, J. (1958). *The growth of logical thinking.* New York: Basic Books.

Jira, D. K., McCloskey, M., and Green, B. F. (1981). Students' misconceptions about motion. *Problem Solving, 2*(12), 3-7.

Kilpatrick, J. (1982, February). What is a problem? *Problem Solving, 4*(2), 1-5.

Kirkland, E. R. (1981). The feasibility of the use of dimensional analysis as a quantitative problem-solving technique in high school physics. *Dissertation Abstracts International, 42*, 2641A. (University Microfilms No. 8115946)

Landry, P., and Moore, R. (1980). A note on problems. *Problem Solving, 2*(3), 5-6.

Larkin, J. H. (1979). Models of skilled and less-skilled problem solving in physics (Tech. Rep.). Pittsburgh: Carnegie-Mellon University.

Lawson, A. E. (1985). A review of research on formal reasoning and science teaching. *Journal of Research in Science Teaching, 22*(7), 569-617.

Layman, J. W. (1983, September). The crisis in high school physics education—Overview of the problem. *Physics Today, 36*(9), 26-30.

Linn, M. C. (1981, April). The role of expectations in complex problem solving. *Problem Solving, 2*(11), 1-8.

NSTA. (1989). Science–Technology–Society: Science education for the 80s. In the *NSTA Handbook 1988-1989* (pp. 162-165). Washington, DC: Author. (Original document adopted 1982; amended 1985)

New York State Department of Education. (1980). *Goals and subgoals for elementary and secondary education.* Albany: New York State Board of Regents.

Poduska, E., and Phillips, D. G. (1986). The performance of college students on Piaget-type tasks dealing with distance, time, and speed. *Journal of Research in Science Teaching, 23*(9), 841-848.

Polya, G. (1957). *How to solve it.* Garden City, NY: Doubleday-Anchor.

Polya, G. (1981). *Mathematical discovery: On understanding learning and teaching problem solving* (Vols. 1 and 2). New York: Wiley.

Reif, F. (1977, June). *Problem-solving skills and human information processing: Some basic issues and practical teaching suggestions.* Paper presented at the meeting of the American Society for Engineering Education, Fargo, ND.

Renner, J. W., Abraham, M. R., and Birnie, H. H. (1986). The occurrence of assimilation and accommodation in learning high school physics. *Journal of Research in Science Teaching, 23*(7), 619-634.

Scheerer, M. (1983, April). Problem solving. *Scientific American, 208,* p. 118.

Shulman, L. S., and Tamir, P. (1973). Research on teaching in the natural sciences in R. M. W. Travers (Ed.), *Second handbook of research on teaching* (pp. 1098-1148). Chicago: Rand McNally.

Snider, R. M. (1966). A project to study the nature of physics teaching using the Flanders method of interaction analysis. (Doctoral dissertation, University of Michigan). *Dissertation Abstracts International, 26,* 7183. (University Microfilms No. ADG60-0678)

Trowbridge, D. E., and McDermott, L. C. (1980, December). An investigation of student understanding of the concept of velocity in one dimension. *American Journal of Physics, 48*(12), 1020-1028.

Trowbridge, D. E., and McDermott, L. C. (1981, March). An investigation of student understanding of the concept of acceleration in one dimension. *American Journal of Physics, 49*(3), 242-253.

True, D. S. (1975). Problem solving instruction in physics. *Dissertation Abstracts International, 35,* 6532A. (University Microfilms No. 75-7856)

Wilson, J. M., and Ingoldsby, T. C. (1983, September). The crisis in physics education: Places where things are right. *Physics Today, 36*(9), 52-58.

Woods, D. R. (1980, June). *Problem solving techniques in physics.* Paper presented at the Congress of the Canadian Association of Physicists, Hamilton, Ontario.

Woods, D. R. (1983). Introducing explicit training in problem solving into our courses. *HERD [Higher Education Research Development], 2*(1), 79-102.

Problem Solving in Biology—
Focus on Genetics

Mike U. Smith
Mercer University School of Medicine
Macon, Georgia

Good teaching in any subject has two central goals: to develop in-depth understanding of that subject and to enhance critical thinking skills. Problem solving requires both: understanding subject content and the ability to apply that understanding.

Biology teachers have long used problem solving to evaluate their students' grasp of biological information and to demonstrate the ability to apply this knowledge to the solution of problems. How could one teach genetics, for example, without solving problems? And doesn't the student who can solve a multiple allele problem understand genetics better than one who can only parrot a definition of the term?

Although biology teachers recognize the importance of problem solving in the curriculum, like teachers in math and the other sciences, they often lose sight of their long-range goals in a nearsighted concentration on correct answers. Researchers in biological education have also been guilty of focusing on final scores that can be averaged and analyzed statistically, rather than on *how* students obtain answers and what clues this process might yield in improving problem solving. Following the lead of math and physics researchers, however, biologists have now begun to investigate the problem-solving process, and these observations have led to suggestions for teaching and learning.

Some of the recent research in problem solving has dealt with such issues as student misconceptions of biological phenomena, the relationships between various measures of individual aptitude and problem-solving success, and the teaching of problem solving to special populations such as the visually impaired (Gough, 1977) and minorities (Fields, 1984). Most of this research has involved studies in classical genetics, although a small sampling of other topics has been considered. These topics include osmosis (Murray, 1983); molecular genetics (Fisher, 1983); metabolism (Leeds, 1986, March); and diffusion, photosynthesis, evolution, and ecology (Marek, 1984, April).

This paper will cover several of the issues explored by research in biological problem solving, particularly in genetics, and their implications for the classroom teacher. For this discussion, a "problem" is any task that requires analysis and reasoning toward a goal (the "solution") (Smith, 1988b, August). Much of what we know about biological problem solving has come from research with genetics problems, using naturalistic clinical interviews. In this technique, which has also been used widely in physics and mathematics, novice and expert problem solvers are asked to think aloud as they solve problems in clinical settings; these interviews are similar to those conducted by J. Piaget. They are essentially "naturalistic" in that the interviewer interrupts only enough to keep the subject talking. (The "novices" in these cases are usually students in introductory courses of the discipline, and the "experts" are Ph.D.s with years of teaching experience.) The recorded interviews are then analyzed carefully for patterns of performance, and the processes of the two groups are compared. Recent research (Smith and Good, 1984b), however, demonstrates that some "novices" are as successful at solving certain moderately difficult problems as are some "experts." This discussion will, therefore, consider the research from the viewpoint of the successful/unsuccessful distinction and will deal primarily with research in genetics.

Successful problem solvers share characteristics that can be grouped under two headings: general problem-solving skills and heuristics (such as breaking the problem into parts) and content-specific understandings and procedures (such as the Punnett square in genetics).

General Problem-Solving Skills

The successful problem solver's performance is unlike that of the unsuccessful problem solver from the very beginning. For example, successful individuals perceive the problem as a task requiring analysis and reason, while the unsuccessful individuals often attempt simply to reproduce remembered pattern (Smith and Good, 1983, April). Unsuccessful individuals are also likely to rely on more general, less powerful heuristics, especially means–ends analysis and trial and error (Smith and Good, 1984a, April; 1984b).

> Pointed nails in shmoos are due to a homozygous recessive allele. What proportion of four-offspring families in which both parent shmoos are heterozygous for pointed nails will have at least two little shmoos that keep ripping their bed sheets? (p. 263)

Individual performances demonstrate the characteristic distinctions between successful and unsuccessful subjects. For example, the following excerpt (Smith, 1983) from a student's unsuccessful attempt at this problem clearly indicates the first behavior noted above; the student attempts to reproduce a remembered pattern rather than applying analysis and reason.

> [STUDENT.] Well, all I remember is, that we had a chart that said when you have, ahm, heterozygous offspring, like it was Ss . . .

Draws.

Ss

I don't even remember what was here. If I . . . I guess it was a [sic] ss that bred with a . . . , oh ssh. I don't remember. But anyway, I remember that the recessive was over here in the corner.

Writes "ss" in the bottom right corner of the Punnett square.

And that it was 1/16 of all the stock.
[INTERVIEWER.] Yeah.
[STUDENT.] And it was, it was when we matched two heterozygote . . .

Successful and unsuccessful problem solvers are also distinguished by their differing abilities in applying logic appropriately. Unsuccessful problem solvers typically use faulty or inexact logic, fail to recognize logical necessity, and do not appear to know the difference between falsifying and weakening a hypothesis (Smith, 1988b, August). They tend to ignore vital assumptions or to apply them without taking exceptions into account. They often make decisions based on opinion or inappropriate evidence, instead of upon the logical arguments and relevant evidence that guide their successful peers.

Unsuccessful individuals (like experts who are attempting problems outside their field) tend to use means–ends analysis. With this procedure, the differences between the present position and the desired state are analyzed, and procedures are chosen to reduce and finally eliminate those differences (Simon and Paige, 1979; Newell, 1980). This strategy has also been called "working backward." Successful individuals, on the other hand, tend to work forward from the conditions given in the problem statement, applying appropriate procedures to derive new data until the desired information is reached. J. H. Larkin (1980, July) calls this the "knowledge development" approach. (See Woods, page 109, for a different interpretation.)

Successful individuals tend to break a problem into a number of parts with which they can deal separately, while unsuccessful individuals try to solve the problem in a single step (Smith and Good, 1984b). In problems of pedigree analysis, for example, unsuccessful individuals often accept the first mode of inheritance that seems to be supported by the pedigree, while successful ones submit the hypothesis to further analysis, test more hypotheses, and use a more complete falsification strategy (Smith, 1986, April; Hackling and Lawrence, 1988). Unsuccessful individuals also show less evidence of planning and pay less attention to detail (Smith and Good, 1984b). And successful individuals, almost without exception, begin to work on the problem as soon as one step in their knowledge development strategy can be performed—well before the entire problem has been read through completely. Unsuccessful individuals typically read the entire problem first, an approach that sometimes appears to confuse them (Smith and Good, 1983, April).

An unsuccessful individual will frequently produce solutions that are incorrect in form or answer questions not asked (Smith and Good, 1984b). For example, a person may produce an answer of "three red to one white" for a problem that asks for the probability that a given offspring will have a given phenotype. This result is particularly interesting because it implies that the subject may not understand the goal of the problem—a serious impediment when using the means–ends approach. After solving a problem, successful individuals are likely to check the problem statement to make sure that the solution satisfies the problem requirements and that it is complete. They are also likely to compare the answer with what they might have expected on the basis of past experience, that is, to ask if the solution seems intuitively correct (Smith and Good, 1983, April).

Content-Specific Knowledge and Procedures

Of all the deficiencies noted in unsuccessful genetics problem solvers, the most frequently reported is a weak understanding of the relationships among the information given in a problem, the Punnett square algorithm, and the cellular events involved (Mertens, 1971; Longden, 1982; Tolman, 1982; Moll and Allen, 1982; Stewart, 1982a; Stewart, 1983; and Costello, 1984). During structured interviews, successful students often offer spontaneous, accurate biological explanations of the events being modeled, while unsuccessful students typically make no attempt to explain the biological events in the problem and become confused because of their poorly integrated biological understanding (Smith and Good, 1984b). B. Longden (1982) observed confusion regarding the definitions of such terms as *gene* and *allele* or *chromosome* and *chromatid*. Unsuccessful students typically do not have a store of common procedures for modeling the genetic events (gametogenesis, random fertilization, etc.); or, if they are familiar with a procedure, such as the Punnett square, they do not understand how it relates to the cellular events and thus cannot modify the problem-solving procedure as needed (Smith and Good, 1983, April). For example, every genetics teacher doubtless has had the experience of seeing a student draw only one allele of one gene in each gamete in a dihybrid cross. One of the principal reasons for doing problem solving in class, in fact, is that the process allows the teacher to identify such gaps in the students' understanding.

Unsuccessful individuals are also less likely to be able to differentiate between essential and nonessential information in the problem statement. For example, during the critical phase of selecting gene symbols, these individuals often choose symbols to represent features that do not distinguish (Smith, 1983). J. H. Stewart's 1983 investigation also reported difficulty with symbol selection and definition. Moreover, unsuccessful individuals are not likely to categorize problems spontaneously, an important part of the solution-planning process (Smith and Good, 1984b).

M. T. H. Chi, P. J. Feltovich, and R. Glaser (1981) have suggested, in fact, that the categorization of a problem in the expert's mind triggers a mass of associated knowledge—both content and process—that can be immediately brought to bear on the problem. This contention is supported by their observations. Experts and novices grouped a set of physics problems into very different types of categories, the former's groupings being based on the "deep structure" of the problem

"This can be solved by applying the law of conservation of energy."

and the others on more superficial structure.

"This looks like a 2 pulley problem."

The superiority of the deep structure is apparent.

The difference between successful and unsuccessful problem solvers regarding content and procedural knowledge is also seen in the recognition and use of patterns. Based on his or her experience with other problems in the content area, the successful individual often searches the problem statement for patterns that he or she has learned to recognize as important clues. The successful solver may, for example, recognize that the genotypes of the parents in a problem constitute a common type of mating known as a testcross, that an approximate ratio of phenotypes in the offspring suggests a known parental genotype combination, or that the pattern of affected individuals in a pedigree indicates a certain type of inheritance. Pattern recognition is often the key to planning the solution path and is sometimes the problem's solution itself. Unsuccessful individuals seem to understand the importance of pattern recognition, but they use patterns in a markedly different and inappropriate manner. Unsuccessful individuals tend to attempt a solution by trying to reproduce various solution patterns from memory (Smith, 1986, April). These patterns, strikingly visual in nature, are applied by beginning physics students (Clement, 1981). The following verbatim exchange (Smith, 1983) demonstrates the problem:

[INTERVIEWER.] Now, I'll just ask you again where you—how you decided the 9:3:3:1 was, was [sic] the numbers you wanted to use.

[STUDENT.] OK. Like this was just a, a [sic] formula that I can remember from class, that we used. And, I hope, seems like this was the case that he used. He crossed a homozygous dominant . . . *(underlines and points to BbCc individual).* This is dominant because the large B and C carry over. Times a homozygous recessive *(points to bbcc individual)* and to check for the different phenotypic and genotypic ratios. So . . .

[INTERVIEWER.] OK, that's what I asked, that it's just something to remember.

[STUDENT.] Yeah. It's a, a formula—a diagram—*(points to Punnett square atempted)* from that class.

The way students use patterns in genetics in similar to the way students use formulas in physics—with some differences. First of all, memorizing $F = ma$ is a much simpler task than memorizing a dihybrid Punnett square. The genetics patterns are, correspondingly, more likely to be incompletely or incorrectly remembered. Second, if the pattern for each slightly different problem constitutes a separate formula, there may be more formulas to memorize in genetics than in physics. Third, as in physics, the experts know the boundary conditions under which it appropriate to apply any given formula; successful problem solvers in genetics also know the boundary conditions under which common patterns apply. This knowledge is strikingly absent in unsuccessful problem solvers.

Within genetics and certain other areas of biology and mathematics, a functional understanding of probability is a prerequisite to solving many problems. Unsuccessful individuals dealing with such problems often demonstrate a deficient understanding of the meanings of fractions, ratios, and probability statements (as, for example, by equating 1:3 with 1 out of 3). Unsuccessful individuals also tend to be unable to apply the product rule to determine the joint probability of two independent events. Biology students are frequently confused when a small sample of offspring fails to conform to an expected ratio. (Some will in fact maintain that it is *impossible* for all four of the offspring of heterozygous parents to be affected by a particular characteristic because the predicted ratio is 3:1.)

One of the more interesting domain-specific observations made in the study of genetics problem solving is that there are points in the process at which solvers can apply one of a number of checks on their work. The most interesting of these checks employs the fact that the sum of all probabilities must equal 1.0. Successful problem solvers often use this check after computing a set of probabilities to make sure that none of the possibilities has been omitted and that the probabilities computed are mathematically correct. The sum of probabilities axiom is remarkably absent in the protocols of unsuccessful individuals. When these people use this sum, it is likely to be as a shortcut instead of a check. Typically, they may use the axiom to determine the last probability in a series by subtracting the sum of the other probabilities from 1.0—a practice that does not contribute to problem-solving success.

In pedigree analysis, the successful solver employs not only procedures and knowledge specific to problem solving in genetics but also procedures that are typical of problem solving in other content areas, especially medical diagnosis. M. W. Hackling and J. Lawrence (1988) and Smith (1986, April) demonstrated independently that the performance of successful problem solvers in this area closely resembles that of adept medical diagnosticians. The process in both cases consists of four phases: cue acquisition, cue interpretation, hypothesis generation, and hypothesis evaluation (Barrows and Tamblyn, 1980). These studies have noted the importance of identifying "critical cues," within the problem statement and/or pedigree, that lead to the generation of a hypothesized mode of inheritance for the trait. The hypothesis is then tested against the remainder of the pedigree, typically by assigning genotypes.

This strategy also parallels that used by chess experts, who have been shown not to consider more moves or a greater depth of move sequences than novices but rather to recognize and consider only those moves that are potentially more fruitful (deGroot, 1966). Hackling and Lawrence reported that the biology teachers they studied recognized more cues that were crucial to the solution of the problem than did the student subjects. In contrast, Smith (1988a) found that successful and unsuccessful individuals identified similar numbers of critical cues, but that the latter group also identified and based decisions upon more than twice as many cues that were not critical.

The cues used in problem solving may best be viewed as the condition side of production rules. Production rules are condition/action pairs. When a condition (cue #1) is recognized as present, the solver knows to take a given action (to test related hypothesis #1). Unsuccessful students make little or no use of such production rules. Typically, the rules they do use are incomplete, lead to no action or to inappropriate action, or are patently incorrect (Smith, 1988a). These differences in the kinds of cues identified by successful and unsuccessful problem solvers and differences in their use of these cues reconfirm the importance of content-specific information and procedures. On the other hand, cue identification and hypothesis testing are powerful general heuristics applicable to a wide variety of problems.

Misconceptions

Researchers have also noted that unsuccessful students are often hampered by their own misconceptions about the subject. The term *misconception* refers to "any conceptual idea whose meaning deviates from the one commonly accepted by scientific consensus" (Cho, Kahle, and Nordland, 1985, p. 707). Some of these misconceptions tend to be shared by many different individuals and to be highly resistant to alteration, at least by conventional teaching methods (Fisher, 1984a). Research in this area has clear implications for classroom teaching in biology.

K. M. Fisher (1984a, 1984b) groups student misconceptions into five general categories. First are ideas that arise out of experiences most people share and that therefore seem intuitively correct to the novice. Although misconceptions are frequently drawn from physics, biology has its share as well. In the field of genetics, for example, students often appear to believe that a gene is dominant if the phenotype it determines is the most frequent in the population, or they may think that a dominant gene will eventually become the most frequent in a population (Fisher, 1984b; Peard, 1983; Tolman, 1982; Smith, 1983). Similarly, Hackling and D. F. Treagust (1982, 1984) report that many of the secondary school students they interviewed believed that the cells of an individual's body are different because different types of cells have different sets of genes. Two studies (Deadman and Kelly, 1978; Kargbo, Hobbs, and Erickson, 1980) have reported that many 7 to 14 year olds believe that one parent (usually the parent of the same sex) contributes more than the other to the phenotype of the offspring. Many college students interviewed believed that a trait observed more commonly in males must be Y-linked (Smith, 1983).

A second group of misconceptions includes errors that occur when the scientific meaning of a term is confused with the common meaning of the same word. For example, Fisher (1984b) reports that subjects often think of dominant *genes* in terms of dominant *people.* Such subjects typically believe that a dominant gene "turns off" a recessive gene.

A third category includes misconceptions that are similar to the understandings of scientists belonging to an earlier period in history, such as those working with Newtonian physics. In biology, elementary school students have been found to believe in both the inheritance of acquired characteristics (Kargbo, Hobbs, and Erickson, 1980) and blended inheritance (Deadman and Kelly, 1978).

A fourth group of misconceptions are those Fisher blames on "the neurological hardware," such as tendencies to associate some words with others. This explanation accounts for certain misconceptions that appear to be remarkably resistant to correction. For example, the persistent confusion of Fisher's students as to whether amino acids are the products or the reactants in protein synthesis appears due at least in part to the fact that these students have developed a stronger semantic connection between the terms *amino acids* and *translation* than between *proteins* and *translation* (Fisher, 1983).

Student misconceptions may also be based on alternate belief systems—Fisher's fifth category. The difficulties that would arise in the study of evolution from a creationist viewpoint are one obvious example. Similarly, Fisher reports that people with certain beliefs about equality, equal opportunity, and self-determination often discount the role of heredity and estimate that it accounts for 15 percent or less of a person's mental characteristics (1984b). M. N. Mahadeva (1983) reports that there is considerable student confusion about the inheritance of intelligence. Some of this confusion may represent the survival of certain beliefs in racial inequality. (Cf. Gould, 1981.)

Some student misconceptions can apparently be traced to teaching techniques. One of the most pervasive of these misconceptions is students' tendency to regard genetic ratios as deterministic rather than probabilistic, that is, to think of the offspring drawn in a Punnett square as actual individuals or numbers of individuals rather than as the probabilities of each genotype appearing among the offspring (Kinnear, 1983; Smith, 1983; Peard, 1983). There appears to be no reason why students would hold this belief prior to instruction. J. F. Kinnear (1983) has observed that her college students demonstrated "an understanding of the independence of successive chance events and of the sensitivity of these chance events to sample size [in real-world problems], but they [the students] used a different set of rules when operating in a genetics context" (p. 88).

This difficulty appears to be related to the students' algorithmic application of the Punnett square (Peard, 1983). Kinnear's 1983 study of problems in genetics from a range of textbooks found that very few of the problems dealt with a small number of offspring and suggested that this limitation contributes to student confusion of the probabilistic nature of genetic ratios. Also, instructors of genetics often draw a Punnett square and casually refer to the genotypic combinations derived as "the four offspring" of the cross instead of "the four types of offspring" or "the four possible gamete combinations." This imprecision probably contributes to students' confusion.

Similarly, T. L. Peard (1983) has reported that his students often maintain that dominant genes for two traits must be linked. Presumably this error is reinforced, if not created, by the instructional use of dihybrid problems in which the dominant traits are always found together in a parent.

Differences Among Individuals

Problem-solving performance is directly affected by a number of individual characteristics such as motivational level, locus of control, cognitive style (Charlton, 1980), field dependence, cognitive development, and academic ability as measured by the Scholastic Aptitude Tests and grade point averages (Yeany, Helpeth, and Barstow, 1980).

As an example, consider field dependence as measured by the Group Embedded Figures Test (Witkin, Oltman, Raskin, and Karp, 1971). Individuals who can "break up an organized visual field in order to keep part of it separate from that field" are field independent (p. 4); individuals who do not have this ability are field dependent. R. R. Ronning, D. McCurdy, and R. Ballinger (1984) observed that, in a group of junior high students, field-independent students outperformed field-dependent students on a selected group of biological problems, most of which would be considered Piagetian tasks appropriate to their age. C. B. Douglass and J. B. Kahle (1978) and Douglass (1979) report similar findings.

Is formal cognitive development a necessary and/or sufficient condition for success in problem solving in genetics? Should we teach genetics to high school students, most of whom have not yet attained the formal level? Unfortunately, the role of cognitive development in success at solving problems in genetics is not clear cut. Many researchers (Walker, Hendrix, and Mertens, 1980; Walker, Mertens, and Hendrix, 1979; Gipson, 1984; Smith, 1983; and Yeany, Helpeth, and Barstow, 1980) have shown a positive correlation between cognitive development and success in problem solving in genetics. S. J. Costello's preliminary factor analysis of genetics problems from a standardized test (1984) has also shown that certain topics in genetics are strongly associated with the Piagetian schemata of proportions, inductive and deductive reasoning, and visualization skills. However, M. H. Gipson's analysis failed to show significant positive correlations between performance on Piagetian tasks that assess development of the schemata of proportional, combinatorial, and probabilistic reasoning and performance on genetics problems intended to require these same reasoning skills.

This apparent contradiction may be partially explained by analyzing the cognitive demands of typical problems in genetics within these three schemata (Smith, 1983). Such problems do not require determining the probability of sequential events *without replacement*—the hallmark of formal operational thought for probabilistic reasoning. Neither do these problems require setting up an equation comparing two ratios, which is the formal operational assessment for proportional reasoning. Some individuals judged to be concrete operational on a combinatorial reasoning task could solve problems in genetics that apparently require combinatorial reasoning at the formal level by properly applying the axiom of the sum of probabilities (Smith, 1983).

Gipson (1984) concludes that because "formal thought is necessary for solving Mendelian genetics problems" (p. 76), we should not teach genetics to preformal students. His study, however, was essentially correlational, and, therefore, it is an insufficient basis for a causal explanation. The case study described above (Smith, 1983), in fact, suggests that formal operational thought is not a necessary (or a sufficient) condition to success. This is not to say that formal thought is not conducive to genetics problem solving, which it clearly is. Peard (1983) blamed his nonformal students' lack of success in solving problems on their "inability to use analytical reasoning, or lack of experience in doing so" (p. 122). It seems appropriate to conclude that formal operational thought is conducive, but not essential, to success in problem solving in genetics. In fact, including genetics in high school might be well advised if it provides the mild disequilibrium known to promote development to the formal level.

Modeling the Problem-Solving Process

Computer modeling of the problem-solving process, developed first in physics, has begun in biology. Stewart and his coworkers at the University of Wisconsin have developed a prototype of a tutoring system called Interactive Genetics Tutor (Collins, 1986, April; Stewart, 1982b; Stewart, Streibel, Collins, and Koedinger, 1986, March). In a related project, Fisher (1988) and her SemNet colleagues at the University of California, Berkeley, are developing a group of extensive semantic network descriptions of the fields of molecular biology, human anatomy, and ecology. This project promises to provide new insights into the complex interrelationships of biological concepts that teachers may fail to make explicit, as well as serve as a basis for further computer models and instructional software. Even before these programs are widely available, the preliminary flow charts (Tolman, 1982; Stewart, 1982b; and Smith, 1983) help break down students' problem-solving tasks into components, subgoals, and specific techniques.

Implications for Teaching and Learning

From the research reviewed above and problem-solving research in other content domains, there emerge many practical suggestions for instructors. Fisher and J. I. Lipson (1983; undated) and Fisher (1984b) offer 17 teaching suggestions to enhance general problem-solving skills:

1. Create safe, supportive, and intellectually challenging environments for learning.
2. Encourage students to make their implicit beliefs explicit and help them to formulate predictions on the basis of their belief systems. [Then, provide opportunity for the students to test their predictions and thus discover the limitations of these beliefs. Encourage students to make this conscious examination of mental mechanisms.]
3. [Make your (i.e., teachers') own] implicit knowledge explicit and available to students. [As teachers, so much of our procedural thought processing has become tacit that we are basically unaware of the extensive automatic processing that goes on in our minds. In order to help students learn to solve problems, we must identify these processes and make them explicit in our instruction.]
4. Present an alternative way of thinking and encourage students to test your mental model. [Once students have realized the inadequacies of their models, the teacher must provide an alternative model that the students can test.]
5. Challenge students repeatedly, providing opportunities for them to test their mental constructs by answering questions, solving problems, or performing in other ways.
6. Provide opportunities for students to practice, practice, practice, with frequent feedback on and discussion of their performance.
7. Design study questions that promote development of problem representations, qualitative judgments about appropriate solution paths, and exploration of the problem space [the individual's understanding of a problem] rather than simply finding correct answers.
8. Present problems which help uncover common student errors.
9. Include many concrete, familiar, and relevant examples in your instruction.
10. Whenever possible, present new information in the form of a story.
11. Emphasize the value of redundancy [repetition] and checking. [Students must learn to routinely monitor their own performance.]
12. Recognize that most or all cognitive errors have multiple causes [and, therefore, that multiple remedial strategies are necessary].
13. Help students develop good metacognitive strategies [thinking about their own ways of thinking and problem solving].
14. Concentrate on promoting deep-level rather than surface-level learning. [For example,] interactive dialogues, in which the novice summarizes, interprets, formulates questions, and makes predictions about a topic, with an expert providing judicious assistance and comment, can facilitate development of the novice's mental model of the domain.
15. Teach in the zone of proximal development [i.e., new information should be clearly related to what the learner already knows].
16. Develop a spiral curriculum [so that] information is acquired in successive approximations.
17. Involve students in the process of science. (Fisher and Lipson, 1983, pp. 150–152; Fisher and Lipson, undated, pp. 34–37; Fisher, 1984b, p. 11)

Content-specific suggestions for biology teachers also emerge from problem-solving research in genetics and other domains. The most frequent recommendations are that the relationships between meiosis and genetics be made explicit and that meiotic events frequently be referred to as explanations of genetic events and algorithms (Tolman, 1982; Peard, 1983; Smith, 1983; Thomson and

Stewart, 1985; Cho, Kahle, and Nordland, 1985). Thomson and Stewart make four specific recommendations:

- emphasizing concepts such as gene, allele, and locus in the discussion of meiosis
- increasing the number and quality of text diagrams that depict meiosis to enhance the understanding of gene, allele, and locus in relation to chromosomes
- continuing, in genetics discussions, to draw chromosomes with alleles on them
- including in the text places where students are expected to draw alternate arrangements of alleles on chromosomes at metaphase I to emphasize the concept of randomness in dihybrid and trihybrid crosses.

These suggestions have led several authors to raise the question of the appropriate sequencing of cell division and genetics (c.f., Tolman, 1982; Mertens, 1971). The more critical issue, however, appears to be making the interrelationships between the two topics clear.

A second group of suggestions centers around the careful use of genetics terms to avoid confusing the students. H. Cho, Kahle, and F. N. Nordland identified improper use of genetics terms in the three most widely used high school biology texts. In this regard, Thomson and Stewart (1985) recommend

1. Reducing the details of meiosis vocabulary (e.g., eliminating concepts such as centrosome, spindle fibers, and asters) so that all vocabulary was related to the replication or division of chromosomes. Eliminating the term *chromatid*. . . . [and using instead the term *duplicated chromosome*].
2. Emphasizing in the meiosis chapter concepts such as gene, allele, and locus, which are normally emphasized only in the genetics chapter. . . .
3. Increasing the number and quality of text diagrams that depict meiosis. . . .
4. Continuing, in the genetics chapter, to draw chromosomes with alleles on them as gamete types are being produced for placement around a Punnett square. . . .
5. Including in the text places where students are expected to draw alternative arrangements of alleles on chromosomes at metaphase I to emphasize the concept of randomness in dihybrid and trihybrid crosses.
6. Using the concepts of gene and allele, trait, and form of a trait consistently so that one concept, such as gene, does not take on the meanings of trait and/or allele.
7. Tying the use of empirical concepts like trait and form to their theoretical equivalents: trait with gene and form with allele. (p. 60)

To prevent students from confusing segregation, diploidy, and dominance, A. Radford and J. A. Bird-Stewart (1982) suggest introducing these three concepts separately using haploid fungi.

Both Kinnear (1983) and Smith (1983) recommend that the probability issues involved in genetics should be addressed directly rather than sidestepped. Avoiding probability appears to encourage students to view genetic ratios deterministically. The research discussed in the preceding section indicates that genetics problems do not normally require formal operational skills in dealing with probability. Many instructors find it difficult to teach problem solving in genetics using probability, and, therefore, they encourage an algorithmic approach to problems. But this opposes two critical instructional goals—understanding the subject in depth and enhancing problem-solving skills—in favor of "getting the right answer."

Similarly, Thomson and Stewart (undated) recognize that teachers must more strongly emphasize the *process* of problem solving, breaking it down into its component parts, and teaching them separately. Thomson and Stewart have developed many problems that ask the student to perform only a single subtask, such as setting up the symbol definition key or identifying gamete types. This approach seems valuable because it helps the student learn to identify problem-solving components, which are often tacit information for the instructor, while it allows the instructor to evaluate the student's progress in each component skill.

These suggestions have not yet been tested by controlled experimentation. In fact, very little experimental work has been done on how to teach to enhance problem-solving skills in biology. F. M. Mele (1978) reported on the advances made by 400 first-year college students not majoring in science, whose teachers used Kaplan's Problem-Solving Biological Curriculum. The experimental group did significantly better than the controls in a post-test on Piagetian concrete/formal operational thought, abstract reasoning, objective/subjective differential reasoning, and critical thinking. R. A. Walker, J. R. Hendrix, and T. R. Mertens (1980) developed a Piagetian programmed instruction guide that beginning college genetics students used for two weeks. The students showed significant gains (at the .01 level) on a problem-solving post-test.

One of the more promising of the recently proposed instructional techniques is the use of microcomputer programs such as CATLAB (Kinnear, 1982a) and BIRDBREED (Kinnear, 1982b). Kinnear (1983) and Peard (1983) used them with promising results. Peard lists several advantages of the technique:
• The computer helps to reveal what the learner knows and what difficulties he or she is having.
• The computer's capacity for generating data randomly permits students to examine levels of knowledge and reasoning rationale in depth.
• The computer makes the student active in his or her own learning.
• The computer requires students to do analytical thinking, both in interpreting unexpected results and in designing experiments for testing hypotheses.
• Computer assessments of weak, missing, or errant concepts can be correlated with those from other sources.
• Students enjoy using the computer.
(Kinnear [1986, April] provides an update on the benefits of using problems developed and presented by the computer.)

In another promising experiment, R. D. Allen and his coworkers (Donovan, 1983; Moll, 1982; Statkiewicz, 1983) developed an introductory biology course "to transmit information efficiently and allow maximum student practice in applying this information" (Moll and Allen, 1982, p. 95). In their course, class time is typically spent viewing and discussing a short videotape of demonstrations, simulations, and experiments. The course emphasizes solving out-of-class exercises and problems by applying the skills learned in class. Students' analytical skills improved, and this improvement was significantly correlated to the student performance on practice problems (Statkiewicz and Allen, 1983). Students could also apply these skills to novel problems.

How I Do It

My own instructional techniques have been shaped by the research discussed in this chapter and by my experience of teaching biology and genetics at both the high school and college levels. The following suggestions have helped my students develop their problem-solving skills.

I suggest that teachers make it clear to students that learning genetics requires problem solving and that it cannot be mastered merely by memorization.

Whenever possible, teachers should relate the subject to real-world phenomena familiar to the students. I often introduce heredity, for example, by talking about a relative who has a rare genetic disease. Male/female ratios in small families (like the students' own) help to address the probabilistic nature of genetic ratios and the effect of small sample size.

Teachers should provide as many hands-on activities as possible. I usually include several coin toss exercises, fruit fly experiments, karyotyping, pop-bead modeling of chromosome behavior, blood typing, personal pedigrees, and other human phenotyping (PTC tasting, red/green color-blindness, etc.). Evidence strongly supports the value of this kind of activity for preformal students (Kamii, 1979).

When discussing problem solving, teachers should emphasize the *process*. I urge beginning students to follow a series of steps that approximate the subgoals identified by Thomson and Stewart (undated) and Smith (1983). This improves the chances of initial success, even if students use the procedures algorithmically at first.

Teachers should allow plenty of time for practice. Some research suggests that the most important factor in problem-solving experience is practice. In E. C. Schuytema, R. Carter, and B. Eshler's 1980 report, practice alone accounted for 89 percent of the difference between success and failure in problem solving.

Before teachers introduce the Punnett square, they should show that the various types of offspring are produced by the combination of each type of egg with every type of sperm. (I use the crisscrossed lines method.) The Punnett square should be introduced as a simple way to model this process in order to identify all possible combinations and not miss any possibilities.

Teachers should model the problem-solving process as they solve demonstration problems. My advice, as teachers model, is to use the following techniques:

• Encourage students to draw an explicit symbol definition key. They often see this as an aid they do not need.

• Ask them to explicitly draw the possible gametes from each parent. Students are tempted to omit this step as well. Experts often do omit it as a separate step because they have learned to do it automatically, but students leaving it out are likely to make errors.

• Draw chromosomes with the appropriate alleles on them in metaphase I frequently to promote a grasp of the relationship between genetics and meiotic events and to show how this arrangement leads to the gametes drawn in a Punnett square.

• Choose problems that allow students to demonstrate typical student misconceptions or errors. Such problems include pedigrees with small numbers of offspring, which help the student to see the difference between probabilistic and genetic deterministic ratios.

• Point out typical student errors. As I solve problems, I frequently stop and ask: "Did I do that correctly?" I sometimes make an error on purpose, so we can discuss why an answer is incorrect. Typical errors include using two different letters for a pair of alleles, omitting the X and Y chromosomes in sex linkage problems, drawing only one allele (letter) in each gamete on a dihybrid cross, and putting gametes from both parents on the same side of the Punnett square. (To discourage the last error, I ask students to draw a circle around the female gametes to suggest an egg and a tailed circle around the males to suggest sperm.)

• Discourage the algorithmic use of the Punnett square. I do so, once the students are adept at simple problems, by introducing problems that require students to modify the algorithm. I might include a testcross (to show that not all ratios are 3:1) and then a cross of a dominant homozygote with a heterozygote or even two homozygotes. In these cases, I ask students to draw only the possible *different* gametes—a familiar instruction by this point. Students who can explain why this situation does not require a 4 x 4 Punnett square have demonstrated a deeper understanding than those who use the square algorithmically.

• Encourage categorization. After students have worked on a few different types of problems (simple dominance, incomplete dominance, multiple allele, dihybrid, etc.), I encourage them to approach each new example by asking "What type of problem is this?" This training encourages students to think about the process of problem solving and to plan a solution strategy.

Recommendations for Further Research

This review of the literature suggests at least four potentially fruitful areas for future research. Most important of these is the validation, by controlled experimental testing, of the teaching suggestions summarized above. These experiments are sometimes hard to set up because of the difficulty of obtaining a random sample from a population and because of the duration of treatment required to achieve measurable differences, but these experiments must be done.

The problem-solving process of successful novices also needs to be investigated further. The apparently very visual nature of novices' problem solving and their infrequent planning calls for examination. The unique processes involved in solving pedigree problems are potentially valuable as well. Stewart and others have already brought us close to computer simulation programs in this area; this development should continue.

The specific role of formal operational thought in problem solving in genetics remains to be elucidated. If the schemata of proportional, combinatorial, and probabilistic reasoning are not critical to genetics problem-solving success, what schemata are important in determining the observed correlation to formal thought? More generally, research on individual differences, their impact on problem-solving performance, and on designing instruction to accommodate individual differences should yield useful information.

A major frontier for researchers may be determining the processes involved in solving complex problems. Such problems often require data analysis, and they will probably closely resemble problem solving as it occurs in the scientist's laboratory—what Ronning, McCurdy, and Ballinger (1984) call "problem solving in 'natural settings.'" A problem from Smith (1983) illustrates the type.

A genetics class was given three pure-breeding stocks of fruit flies:
Stock 1: wild-type eyes
Stock 2: white eyes
Stock 3: white eyes

Students made the following crosses:

Cross of stock 1 females and stock 2 males:
F1= all wild type
F2= (not done)
Cross of stock 1 females and stock 3 males:
F1= all wild type
F2= 9 wild type: 3 brown: 3 red: 1 white, with an equal frequency of each phenotype in males and females
Cross of stock 2 females and stock 1 males:
F1= all wild-type females; all white-eyed males
F2= (not done)
Cross of stock 3 females and stock 1 males:
F1= all wild type
F2= 9 wild type: 3 brown, 3 red, 1 white, with an equal frequency of each phenotype in both males and females
Cross of stock 2 females and stock 3 males:
F1= all wild-type females; all white-eyed males
F2= 9 wild type: 3 brown: 3 red: 17 white, with an equal frequency of each phenotype in both males and females
Cross of stock 3 females and stock 2 males:
F1= all wild type, both males and females
F2 females= 9 wild type: 3 brown: 3 red: 1 white
F2 males= 9 wild type: 3 brown: 3 red: 17 white

What is the complete genotype of each stock, 1, 2, and 3?
Explain the results of this set of crosses.

An even more interesting variation of this problem would be one in which actual raw data are presented, in the form of offspring counts, instead of the idealized ratios.

Stewart's 1983 research proposes studying the influence of different types of student evaluation on what he calls "meaningful learning." In genetics, for example, what would be the effect of evaluation instruments that required students to justify their answers to problems conceptually? Would meaningful learning increase if testing rewarded more than the application of an algorithm? The work of Allen and his colleagues has clearly begun this study, but greater attention should be focused on its development.

References

Barrows, H. S., and Tamblyn, R. M. (1980). *Problem-based learning—An approach to medical education.* New York: Springer.

Charlton, R. E. (1980). Cognitive style considerations for the improvement of biology education. *American Biology Teacher, 42,* 244-247, 260.

Chi, M. T. H., Feltovich, P. J., and Glaser, R. (1981). Categorization and representation of physics problems by experts and novices. *Cognitive Science, 5,* 121-152.

Cho, H., Kahle, J. B., and Nordland, F. N. (1985). An investigation of high school biology textbooks as sources of misconceptions and difficulties in genetics, and some suggestions for teaching genetics. *Science Education, 69,* 707-719.

Clement, J. J. (1981). Solving problems with formulas: Some limitations. *Engineering Education, 72,* 158-162.

Collins, A. (1986, April). *Problem-solving rules for genetics.* Paper presented at the meeting of the National Association for Research in Science Teaching, New Orleans.

Costello, S. J. (1984). *The relationships among logical and spatial skills and understanding genetics concepts and problems.* Princeton, NJ: Educational Testing Service.

Deadman, J. A., and Kelly, P. J. (1978). What do secondary school boys understand about evolution and heredity before they are taught the topics? *Journal of Biological Education, 12,* 7-15.

DeGroot, A. D. (1966). Perception and memory versus thought: Some old ideas and recent findings. In B. Kleinmutz (Ed.), *Problem solving: Research, method, and theory* (pp. 19-50). New York: John Wiley and Sons.

Donovan, M. P., and Allen, R. D. (1983). *Analytical problems in biology.* Minneapolis, MN: Burgess.

Douglass, C. B. (1979). Making biology easier to understand. *American Biology Teacher, 41,* 277-281.

Douglass, C. B., and Kahle, J. B. (1978). The effects of instructional sequence and cognitive style on the achievement of high school biology students. *Journal for Research in Science Teaching, 15,* 407-412.

Fields, L. (1984). Evaluation of a university biology course designed to promote development of logical reasoning skills in educationally disadvantaged minority students planning careers in health care professions. *Dissertation Abstracts International, 45/01,* 93A. (University Microfilms No. DA 840406)

Fisher, K. M. (1983). Amino acids and translation: A misconception in biology. In H. Helm and J. D. Novak (Eds.), *Proceedings of the International Seminar on Misconceptions in Science and Mathematics* (pp. 407-419). Ithaca, NY: Cornell University Department of Education.

Fisher, K. M. (1984a). *A misconception in biology: Amino acids and translation.* Davis: University of California Press.

Fisher, K. M. (1984b). *Student misconceptions and teacher assumptions in college biology.* Paper presented at the Symposium on Cognitive Development and Disciplinary Knowledge at the meeting of American Association for the Advancement of Science, New York.

Fisher, K. M. (1988, April). *SemNet: Software for student or faculty construction of large relational networks of concepts.* Paper presented at the meeting of the American Educational Research Association, New Orleans.

Fisher, K. M., and Lipson, J. I. (1983). Ten rules of thumb: Information-processing interpretations of error research in learning. In H. Helm and J. D. Novak (Eds.), *Proceedings of the the International Seminar on Misconceptions in Science and Mathematics* (pp. 150-152). Ithaca, NY: Cornel University Department of Education.

Fisher, K. M., and Lipson, J. I. (Undated). *Information-processing interpretations of errors in college science and mathematics learning.* Davis, CA: University of California.

Gipson, M. H. (1984). Relationships between formal operational thought and conceptual difficulties in genetics problem solving (Doctoral dissertation, University of Oklahoma). *Dissertation Abstracts International, 45/12,* 3600A. (University Microfilms No. DA 8504321)

Gough, E. R. (1977). The science-related problem-solving processes of visually impaired adolescents. *Dissertation Abstracts International, 38/06A,* 3399A. (University Microfilms No. DDJ77-27000)

Gould, S. J. (1981). *The mismeasure of man.* New York: W. W. Norton.

Hackling, M. W., and Lawrence, J. (1988). Expert and novice solutions of genetic pedigree problems. *Journal of Research in Science Teaching, 25,* 531–546.

Hackling, M. W., and Treagust, D. F. (1982). What lower secondary students should understand about the mechanisms of inheritance and what they do understand following instruction. *Research in Science Education, 12,* 78–88.

Hackling, M. W., and Treagust, D. F. (1984). Research data necessary for meaningful review of grade ten high school genetics curricula. *Journal of Research in Science Teaching, 21,* 197–209.

Kamii, C. (1979). Teaching for thinking and creativity: A Piagetian view. In A. E. Lawson (Ed.), *The psychology of teaching for thinking and creativity* (pp. 29–58). (1980 Association for Education of Teachers of Science Yearbook.) Columbus, OH: ERIC Clearinghouse for Science, Mathematics, and Environmental Education.

Kargbo, D. B., Hobbs, E. D., and Erickson, G. L. (1980). Children's beliefs about inherited characteristics. *Journal of Biological Education, 14,* 137–146.

Kinnear, J. F. (1982a). *CATLAB* [Computer program]. Iowa City: CONDUIT.

Kinnear, J. F. (1982b). *BIRDBREED* [Computer program]. Boston: EduTech.

Kinnear, J. F. (1983). Identification of misconceptions in genetics and the use of computer simulations in their correction. In H. Helm and J. D. Novak (Eds.), *Proceedings of the International Seminar on Misconceptions in Science and Mathematics* (pp. 84–92). Ithaca, NY: Cornell University Department of Education.

Kinnear, J. F. (1986, April). *Computer simulation and problem solving in genetics.* Paper presented at the meeting of the American Educational Research Association, San Francisco.

Larkin, J. H. (1980, July). *Enriching formal knowledge: A model for learning to solve textbook physics problems* (Tech. Rep.). Pittsburgh: Carnegie-Mellon University.

Leeds, M. J. (1986, March). *Characterizing quantitative mental models of learners about energy metabolism.* Paper presented at the meeting of the National Association for Research in Science Teaching, San Francisco.

Longden, B. (1982). Genetics—Are there inherent learning difficulties? *Journal of Biological Education, 16,* 135–139.

Mahadeva, M. N. (1983). Misconceptions and myths masquerading as biological facts. In H. Helm and J. D. Novak (Eds.), *Proceedings of the International Seminar on Misconceptions in Science and Mathematics* (pp. 266–271). Ithaca, NY: Cornell University Department of Education.

Marek, E. A. (1984, April). *Concept understandings and misunderstandings of high school biology students.* Paper presented at the meeting of the National Association for Research in Science Teaching, New Orleans.

Mele, F. M. (1978). A biology problem-solving program's effect on college students' transition from concrete to formal thought. *Dissertation Abstracts International, 38/12A,* 7290A. (University Microfilms No. DDJ78-09010)

Mertens, T. R. (1971). On teaching meiosis and Mendelism. *American Biology Teacher, 33,* 430–431.

Moll, M. B., and Allen, R. D. (1982). Developing critical thinking skills in biology. *Journal of College Science Teaching, 12,* 95–98.

Murray, D. L. (1983). Misconceptions of osmosis. In H. Helm and J. D. Novak (Eds.), *Proceedings of the International Seminar on Misconceptions in Science and Mathematics* (pp. 428–433). Ithaca, NY: Cornell University Department of Education.

Newell, A. (1980). One final word. In D. Tuma and F. Reif (Eds.), *Problem-solving and education: Issues in teaching and research* (pp. 175–189). Hillsdale, NJ: Lawrence Erlbaum Associates.

Peard, T. L. (1983). The microcomputer in cognitive development research (or, Putting the byte on misconceptions). In H. Helm and J. D. Novak (Eds.), *Proceedings of the International Seminar on Misconceptions in Science and Mathematics* (pp. 112–123). Ithaca, NY: Cornell University Department of Education.

Radford, A., and Bird-Stewart, J. A. (1982). Teaching genetics in schools. *Journal of Biological Education, 16,* 177–180.

Ronning, R. R., McCurdy, D., and Ballinger, R. (1984). Individual differences: A third component in problem-solving instruction. *Journal of Research in Science Teaching, 21,* 71–82.

Schuytema, E. C., Carter, R., and Eshler, B. (1980, April). *Development and evaluation of problem-solving skills in microbiology.* Paper presented at the meeting of the American Educational Research Association, Boston.

Simon, H. A., and Paige, J. M. (1979). Cognitive processes in solving algebra word problems. In H. A. Simon (Ed.), *Models of thought.* New Haven: Yale University Press.

Smith, M. U. (1983). A comparative analysis of the performance of experts and novices while solving selected classical genetics problems (Doctoral dissertation, Florida State University). *Dissertation Abstracts International, 44/02,* 451A. (University Microfilms No. 8314200)

Smith, M. U. (1986, April). *Problem solving in classical genetics: Successful and unsuccessful pedigree analysis.* Paper presented at the meeting of the American Educational Research Association, San Francisco.

Smith, M. U. (1988a). Successful and unsuccessful problem solving in classical genetic pedigrees. *Journal of Research in Science Teaching, 25,* 411–433.

Smith, M. U. (1988b, August). *Toward a unified theory of problem solving: A response from genetics research.* Paper presented at the annual meeting of the Cognitive Science Society, Montreal.

Smith, M. U., and Good, R. (1983, April). *A comparative analysis of the performance of experts and novices while solving selected classical genetics problems.* Paper presented at the meeting of the National Association for Research in Science Teaching, Dallas.

Smith, M. U., and Good, R. (1984a, April). *A proposed developmental sequence for problem-solving ability in classical genetics: The trial-and-error to deductive logic continuum.* Paper presented at the meeting of the National Association for Research in Science Teaching, Dallas.

Smith, M. U., and Good, R. (1984b). Problem solving and classical genetics: Successful versus unsuccessful performance. *Journal of Research in Science Teaching, 21,* 895–912.

Statkiewicz, W. R., and Allen, R. D. (1983, February). Practice exercises to develop critical thinking skills. *Journal of College Science Teaching, 12(4),* 262–266.

Stewart, J. H. (1982a). Difficulties experienced by high school students when learning basic Mendelian genetics. *American Biology Teacher, 44,* 80–89.

Stewart, J. H. (1982b). Two aspects of meaningful problem solving in science. *Science Education, 66,* 731–749.

Stewart, J. H. (1983). Student problem solving in high school genetics. *Science Education, 67,* 523–540.

Stewart, J. H., Streibel, M., Collins, A., and Koedinger, K. (1986, March). *The Genetics Tutorial Project: Combining educational research, expert systems, and instructional software.* Paper presented at the meeting of the National Association for Research in Science Teaching, San Francisco.

Thomson, N., and Stewart, J. (Undated). *Meaningful algorithms for secondary school genetics instruction.* Unpublished manuscript, University of Wisconsin, Madison.

Thomson, N., and Stewart, J. (1985). Secondary school genetics instruction: Making problem solving explicit and meaningful. *Journal of Biological Education, 19,* 53–62.

Tolman, R. R. (1982). Difficulties in genetics problem solving. *American Biology Teacher, 44,* 425–527.

Walker, R. A., Hendrix, J. R., and Mertens, T. R. (1980). Sequenced instruction in genetics and Piagetian cognitive development. *American Biology Teacher, 42,* 104–108.

Walker, R. A., Mertens, T. R., and Hendrix, J. R. (1979, January). Formal operational reasoning patterns and scholastic achievement in genetics. *Journal of College Science Teaching, 8(3)* 156–61.

Witkin, H. A., Oltman, P. K., Raskin, E., and Karp, S. A. (1971). Group embedded figures test. Palo Alto, CA: Consulting Psychologists Press.

Yeany, R. H., Helpeth, E. A., Jr., and Barstow, W. E. (1980, April). *Interactive instructional videotapes, scholastic aptitude, cognitive development, and locus of control as variables influencing science achievement.* Paper presented at the meeting of the National Association for Research in Science Teaching, Boston.

Problem Solving in Chemistry

Dorothy L. Gabel
Indiana University—Bloomington

Chemistry teachers would like their students to become excellent problem solvers. Yet most students find problem solving one of the most frustrating aspects of their introductory chemistry courses. Lack of success in solving problems probably discourages many students from taking any chemistry courses after their first.

What does research tell us about the process of problem solving in chemistry? Why do many students have a difficult time solving chemistry problems? Are there effective ways of teaching problem solving?

Defining the Problem and the Problem-Solving Process

Before we address the other questions we must define the term *chemistry problem*. Examine the following statements. Which of them would you define as chemistry problems?

1. The formula for density is mass/volume. If the mass of an unknown material is 15 grams and its volume is 8 grams, calculate its density.
2. Consider two substances, A and B. The density of substance A is greater than the density of substance B. A sample of A and a sample of B have the same mass. Which sample has the larger volume?
3. For normal lemonade, 40 grams of lemonade powder are dissolved in one liter of water. What would be the concentration if 80 grams of lemonade powder were added to two liters of water and then the water was evaporated until one liter remained?
4. A sample of methane gas (CH_4) has a mass of 32 grams. How many molecules of methane are in the sample?

There are many different definitions of *problem* in use today. Some would call the first statement above an exercise rather than a problem. All the information to arrive at a solution is given in the problem, so the student must only apply an algorithm to arrive at the correct answer. Statement 2 does not contain numbers. Must a problem contain numbers? Statement 3 contains numbers, but is concerned with lemonade, not the chemical species normally used in courses. Statement 4 is typical of what most chemistry teachers would call a problem.

For the purposes of this review, however, all four of these examples will be considered problems. The definition of a problem will be that of J. R. Hayes (1981), who says that a problem exists when a person perceives a gap between where he or she is and where he or she wants to be but doesn't know how to cross the gap. Even though the first problem can be solved with an algorithm, many students find it difficult to apply such algorithms. The student who can solve the second problem knows more chemistry than one who can only solve the first. Problem 3 is analogous to typical molarity problems that many students find very difficult. Can beginning chemistry students solve such problems if they contain familiar substances?

Problem solving in any area is a complex process. It involves an understanding of the language in which the problem is stated, an interpretation of what information is given and what is sought, an understanding of the concepts involved in the solution, and in some cases the ability to perform mathematical operations. R. E. Mayer's 1982 description of the types of knowledge needed to solve math problems covers similar ground and is largely applicable to problem solving in chemistry. According to Mayer, a successful problem solver must first be able to represent the problem, which requires linguistic, factual, and schematic knowledge. Solving it requires algorithmic and strategic knowledge as well.

This review will present research findings that focus on the components of the chemistry problem-solving process, the role of student knowledge and aptitudes in problem solving, and some strategies for teaching problem solving. No attempt will be made to include every research report published on the subject.

Linguistic and In-Task Variables in Problem Solving

The first step in successful problem solving is to understand the meaning of the problem. This requires knowing the vocabulary in which the problem is stated and its syntax. Two types of words occur in problems: ordinary words science teachers generally expect students to know already and technical terms, such as *mole* and *density*, which involve concepts specific to the discipline. The first question, therefore, that needs to be asked in teaching problem solving is, "Do the students understand the statement of the problem?"

In England, J. R. T. Cassels and A. H. Johnstone (1984, 1985) studied student understanding of science classroom vocabulary. They found that when they simplified the key words in questions, substantially greater numbers of students were able to answer correctly. For example, 7 percent more students could answer the question, "Which of the following is a choking gas?" than could answer "Which . . . is a pungent gas?". If quantitative questions were changed from "least" to "most," there was also an increase in success rates. Successful answers increased by 26 percent when that substitution was made in this question: "Which of the following solutions of a salt in water is the least concentrated?" Cassels and Johnstone report similar results after changing other negative forms to positive, after simplifying long and complex questions, and after shifting passive voice to active.

Cassels and Johnstone's testing also produced an extensive list of rather common words that British students at various levels did not understand outside of a restricted context. Some of these are *concept, contrast, displace, diversity, factor, fundamental, incident, negligible, relevant, relative, spontaneous,* and *valid.* Because there is no reason to suspect that students in the United States have a better grasp of vocabulary and usage than their British counterparts, some of students' problem-solving difficulties probably stem from these linguistic variables.

D. L. Gabel and R. D. Sherwood (1984) sought to determine the importance of several other in-task variables by using analogy problems modeled after moles problems but using familiar substances such as sugar and oranges. The researchers asked the following questions:

- Are problems easier to solve when the particles are large—for example, oranges rather than grains of sugar?

    No differences were found.

- Are problems easier to solve when they involve even multiples of the standards rather than fractional parts? (If a dozen oranges weighed 4 pounds, would students be able to find the volume of 24 pounds more easily than the volume of 2 pounds?)

    Students found problems with even multiples easier, although they were allowed to use a calculator to solve the problems.

- Are problems easier to solve if, for instance, the word *bag* is substituted for the word *billion?*

    No differences.

- Are problems easier to solve if the numeral *1* is used instead of *one, a,* or *an?*

    Yes, using the numeral makes the problem easier.

- Are problems requiring multiplication easier to solve than those requiring division?

    Yes.

    T. H. Falls and B. Voss (1985, April) found that the presence of certain in-task variables made problems difficult to solve for field-dependent students.[*] Field-independent students were more capable of isolating the relevant information in a problem that contained both relevant and irrelevant data. These students were also more successful in solving problems containing a direct logic task and requiring the algebraic format $A = KB$.

    All four studies highlight the impact of problem presentation on student success. This factor operates quite apart from how well students understand the science concepts involved in problems and the algorithms and strategies needed to solve them.

Concept Development as a Variable

One major reason beginning chemistry students fail to solve problems is that they do not grasp the concepts involved: Their knowledge base is inadequate. This difficulty has been shown by four studies in which students were asked to think aloud as they attempted to solve problems: S. C. Nurrenbern, 1979; H. Kramers-Pals, J. Lambrechts, and P. J. Wolff, 1982; Gabel, Sherwood, and L. G. Enochs, 1984; and T. J. Greenbowe, 1984. Greenbowe's study, in addition to analyzing the problem-solving skills of novice chemistry students, compared novice problem solving with that of experts. He found that the experts had a greater grasp of the concepts and thus were able to represent problems more accurately and completely. Previous expert/novice studies in biology and physics have demonstrated that experts not only have a superior command of concepts but are also able to retrieve the concepts easily from long-term memory because they are linked in a conceptual framework.

    In order for students to become expert problem solvers, then, they must master the concepts upon which problems are based and link them together in a system. Johnstone (1983) concludes that problem-solving success depends on three interrelated factors:

- the size of the information content of the problem
- the problem solver's level of conceptual development and integration
- the degree of difficulty perceived by the problem solver

    Students with high concept development can cope with difficult, high infor-

---

[*]This concept is used here as it was in M. U. Smith's paper in this volume. Smith summarizes: "Consider field dependence as measured by the Group Embedded Figures Test (Witkin, Oltman, Raskin, and Karp, 1971). Individuals who can 'break up an organized visual field in order to keep part of it separate from that field' are field independent (p. 4); individuals who do not have this ability are field dependent."

mation problems. Others will be successful only with those that contain little information.

Mass and Volume

Enochs and Gabel (1984) found that even college students who had taken high school chemistry were unable to find the volume of objects other than rectangular solids. Students applied the formula *volume = length x width x height* to objects of any geometric shape. A. B. Champagne, L. E. Klopfer, and S. Chaiklin (1984, April) explain students' failure to distinguish between two fundamental properties of matter, mass and volume, by the fact that the two vary in an identical way; that is, as the mass of an object doubles, its volume also doubles. Champagne et al also contend that students do not understand concepts such as volume because the concepts are not taught in a variety of contexts. For example, if students are asked to obtain the volume of a bottle, are they supposed to find the volume of glass in the bottle or only its capacity. Because many students believe from previous experience that water is absorbed by sand, when asked to predict the new volume when 50 mL of sand is poured into a 1000 mL graduated cylinder containing 200 mL of water, they may guess that the water level will be below the 200 mL mark. Poorly developed concepts of mass and volume—the fundamentals of stoichiometric relationships—taught in an insufficient variety of contexts hinder students from solving chemistry problems in a meaningful way.

States of Matter

Concepts that are also fundamental to the understanding of chemistry are the states of matter and the changes of state that matter undergoes. D. L. Shepherd and J. W. Renner in 1982 found that many 12th-grade students had misconceptions about the states of matter. R. J. Osborne and M. M. Cosgrove (1983) surveyed students in New Zealand on their conceptions of what happens when water changes state. They found that 40 percent of the 17-year-old students thought the large bubbles in boiling water were made of oxygen and hydrogen instead of steam. Thirty percent thought that when a wet dish dried, the water went off as oxygen and hydrogen. And when asked where the drops on the outside of a jar of cold water came from, about 35 percent of the students said from oxygen and hydrogen.

Heat and Temperature

Although heat and temperature are not as fundamental to chemistry as mass, volume, and the states of matter, they are also fundamental concepts. Studies by E. Albert (1978), G. L. Erickson (1979, 1980), and M. Shayer and H. Wylam (1981) found that children under the age of 13 had misconceptions about these two concepts. Research has not been done on whether these misconceptions persist for students who enroll in introductory chemistry, but this is very likely the case, because these topics are seldom treated in any formal way outside of chemistry or physics courses.

Mole Concept

In addition to the fundamental properties of matter, which chemistry teachers frequently assume that students already know, there are other concepts which contribute to the basis of chemical calculations. One of these is the mole.

The first thing that research tells us about the mole concept is that students in many parts of the world have difficulty with it. I. M. Duncan and Johnstone (1973) question whether the topic is even appropriate for 15 year olds, since their studies indicate that only about 40 percent of 15-year-old Scottish students are at the Piagetian formal operational stage. Although the students tested had little difficulty calculating the gram formula weight of compounds, they failed to understand the meaning of the coefficients in balanced chemical equations and consequently interpreted all relationships between chemicals in a reaction as 1:1. They also had difficulty solving molarity problems.

S. Novick and J. Menis (1976) studied Israeli 15 year olds' understanding of the mole concept, finding that even students with above-average mental ability (as measured by IQ scores of 100–122) had less than a satisfactory grasp of the concept. The mean score on an interview test was only 64 percent. For students with IQs from 86 to 100, it was 35 percent. Novick and Menis concluded that few students view the mole as a counting number and that many do not restrict the molar volume of 22.4 liters to gases.

R. Cervellati, A. Montuschi, D. Perugini, N. Grimellini-Tomasini, and B. P. Balandi found in 1982 that Italian students beginning college chemistry, all of whom had taken high school chemistry, varied in their mastery according to the type of high school they had attended. They found the students generally unfamiliar with the mole as a unit of the amount of substance. Although the value 22.4 liters at standard temperature and pressure was familiar to students, they could not relate it to pressure, temperature, or state.

U.S. students have the same difficulties. Gabel (1981), who listened to 72 students solving mole problems aloud, found that they frequently confused moles with molecules and generally lacked the conceptual base to solve problems meaningfully. Very few students could define the mole correctly as an amount of substance that has mass and volume and consists of 6.02×10^{23} particles.

One reason students have such difficulty solving mole problems is that the solution involves piecing together a large number of concepts and relating them to one another. Sometimes teachers fail to recognize the complexity of this matrix of concepts. D. M. Gower, D. J. Daniels, and G. Lloyd (1977a, 1977b) and A. K. Griffiths, H. Kass, and A. G. Cornish (1983) have validated learning hierarchies for the mole concept. Griffiths' team found that the key skill in learning the mole concept was the ability to relate masses of substance in terms of the relative number of particles—to calculate the actual number of particles in a given mole and the mass quantities of substances. The team also suggests that students should learn to relate the masses of different substances before working with particle relationships.

Particulate Nature of Matter

Introductory chemistry students can also have difficulty solving problems if they do not understand the particulate nature of matter. How can students solve molarity problems that involve raising the concentration of solutions if they cannot form a mental representation of the process?

Mounting evidence suggests that students lack a conceptual framework for the particulate nature of matter. Novick and J. Nussbaum (1978) found that, although 60 percent of Israeli students in grade eight (ages 14–15) consistently used a particle model to explain phenomena involving gases, only 46 percent were confident that there was empty space among the particles. In a 1981 study of students of different ages, Novick and Nussbaum were concerned with five facts about the particle model. The percentage of the junior high students who understood each concept follows in parentheses.
- Gas particles are uniformly distributed (70 percent).
- Gas particles are in constant motion (30 percent).
- Heating and cooling cause changes in particle motion (50 percent).
- Liquefaction involves a change in particle density (70 percent).
- There is empty space between [sic] the particles of a gas (50 percent).

The above studies examined students' overall perceptions of the particulate nature of matter. B. Eylon, R. Ben-Zvi, and J. Silberstein (1982, April, part I) examined students' views of specific molecules. They found that, among students who had six months of chemistry, 94 percent realized that O_2 consists of two atoms bonded together, but only 64 percent could correctly describe the molecule N_2O_4. They concluded that students formed an additive rather than an interactive view of structure, and viewed compounds as made of fragments rather than as new entities in composition reactions. The same authors reported in a separate study (1982, April, part II) that, when students were asked to sketch representative chemical species such as O_2 as solids, liquids, and gases, from 23 to 30 percent pictured only one molecule. Eylon, Ben-Zvi, and Silberstein recommend that teachers working with molecular models represent the structure and processes with separate particles, rather than with unitary molecules.

W. L. Yarroch (1985) found similar results when she interviewed 14 high school students on how they balanced simple chemical equations. All the students were able to balance the four equations they were given, but half of them were unable to construct diagrams consistent with the notation of the balanced equations. Their diagrams were consistent with the total number of atoms being conserved, but did not represent the individual species correctly. For example, a representation for the reaction of

$$N_2 + 3H_2 \longleftrightarrow 2NH_3$$

might be

$$(N)(N) + (H)(H)\ (H)(H)\ (H)(H) \longleftrightarrow (N)(N)(H)(H)(H)(H)(H)(H)$$

Gabel, D. Hunn, and K. V. Samuel (1987) asked elementary education majors to draw sketches representing the particles in solids, liquids, and gases, and the realignments or interactions of these particles in changes in state or chemical reactions. Students who had taken chemistry scored only slightly higher than students who had not. Research in physics instruction indicates that misconceptions are equally tenacious in other scientific fields.

By the time students enroll in a formal course in chemistry they have already acquired misconceptions about some of the fundamental concepts they need to solve chemistry problems. Although these misconceptions hinder learning, they are positive evidence of the effort we all exert from an early age to make sense of the world. Research by W. de Vos and A. H. Verdonk (1987) corroborates the survival of misconceptions in students trying to understand certain chemical properties. De Vos and Verdonk found that chemistry students frequently attribute properties to *individual* molecules (actually due to the *collection* of molecules). For example, one group of students trying to explain glue's action decided that each "glue molecule" was covered with something sticky; other students said that, in liquids like water and alcohol, molecules cannot be solid objects but must be "tiny little droplets."

Naive alternative frameworks tend to fall into common patterns. A teacher who is aware of these common misconceptions can formulate instruction that begins where the students are. For example, students may be asked to compare by touch the temperatures of a piece of metal and a piece of paper in a 70-degree room. The metal will seem colder. Placing a thermometer on the surfaces of the two materials and reading identical temperatures may impress a student with the importance of objective measurement.

If students' problem-solving skills in chemistry are to improve, chemistry teachers will need to spend much more time on concept acquisition. One way to do so is to use hands-on activities to present each concept in a variety of contexts. This approach alone, however, does not guarantee that students will use the concepts when appropriate. D. M. Bunce and Gabel (1989, April) found that, while many students who solve problems by using algorithms understood the underlying concepts, the students did not draw upon this conceptual knowledge in solving problems involving stoichiometry and gas laws. M. E. Brenner (1989, March) reports a similar situation with young children who learn to spend and save cash in the marketplace but do not connect this experience with what they learn about money values at school. Teachers must make efforts to reinforce students' acquisition of concepts by including qualitative conceptual questions on tests and rewarding correct answers. In addition, when problems appear on tests, teachers must allow students enough time to solve them using a conceptual method rather than the less time-consuming algorithmic approach.

Aptitude Research

For more than 10 years, science educators have been examining the relationship between student aptitude and problem-solving ability. Researchers (Wheeler and Kass, 1977, March; Nurrenbern, 1979; Gabel and Sherwood, 1983; and Falls and Voss, 1985, April) have all linked problem solving to proportional reasoning. Therefore, if it were possible to improve students' proportional reasoning ability, their chemistry problem solving could be expected to improve accordingly. Unfortunately, A. E. Wheeler and H. Kass (1977) found proportional reasoning ability resistant to improvement through instruction. H. Williams, C. W. Turner, L. Debreuil, J. Fast, and J. Berestiansky (1979) found that while third-year college students were generally superior to first-year students in proportional reasoning, the freshmen outperformed their elders on some key items, such as modifying a recipe.

Gabel, Sherwood, and Enochs (1984) observed how students with varying proportional reasoning abilities solved problems aloud. They listened to more than 200 students solving chemistry problems and found that students with high proportional reasoning ability answered correctly more often and used reasoning strategies more effectively than did students of low proportional reasoning ability.

In a detailed 1979 study of the oral problem-solving performance of concrete and formal operational high school chemistry students, Nurrenbern found few differences between those two groups. Formal students were somewhat better at reading, organizing, and evaluating problems, but the groups were similar in their use of reasoning, in recall techniques, in the number of chemistry errors, in the strategies selected to solve stoichiometric problems, and in their perception of relationships between the chemistry classroom and the outside world.

C. R. Ward and J. D. Herron (1980), however, found that formal operational college chemistry students performed better, not only with formal chemistry tasks but also with concrete materials. The two groups were similar only in dealing with content that required mere memorization of facts and formulas. Research has also probed the relationship of chemistry problem solving to several other aptitudes. F. H. Squires (1977) and Falls and Voss (1985, April) related problem solving to field dependence and field independence. Squires found field-independent eighth graders better at solving science problems; Falls and Voss determined the same for high school chemistry students. Field-independent students were significantly better at solving proportional reasoning problems containing relevant and irrelevant information and/or implicit information. Field independence may, in fact, be defined as a measure of how well an individual can restructure a problem to make it personally meaningful.

Another aptitude that may be related to problem-solving ability is skill at visualization. C. S. Carter, A. LaRussa, and G. M. Bodner (1985, April) found that college chemistry students of high visualization ability outperformed students of low visualization ability on problem-solving and quantitative tasks.

Implications for Instruction

Having seen some reasons why introductory chemistry students have difficulty solving problems—linguistic and other in-task variables, differences in concept development, and differences in aptitude—we may consider instructional strategies that can help students to become better problem solvers.

There is no single best technique. Although many chemistry teachers and most introductory texts teach problem solving by the factor label method, Gabel and Sherwood (1983) have shown that this method is not the best approach for all students. They found that high school students with high math anxiety and low proportional reasoning ability achieve more on problems involving moles, molarity, and stoichiometry if they are provided with analogies and schematic diagrams. The diagram that was used in this study is shown in Figure 1.

Figure 1: *Schematic Diagram for Solving Stoichiometry Problems*

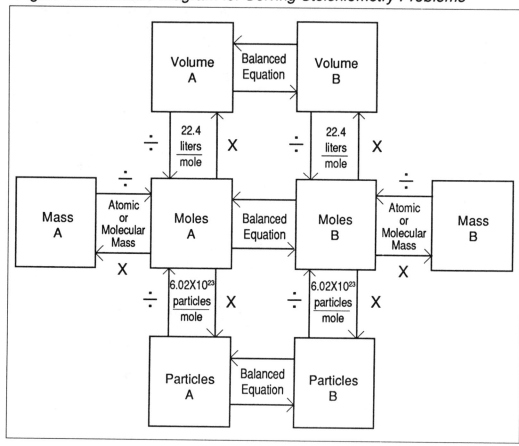

The analogies were those commonly used in chemistry instruction, such as comparing a mole to a dozen and using pieces of fruit to represent chemical species. Further research by Gabel and Samuel (1986), however, suggests that analogies are not helpful with certain kinds of problems. In this study 619 high school chemistry students were asked to solve molarity problems and analogous lemonade problems. An example of a pair of problems follows:

Molarity Problem: How many grams of sodium hydroxide (NaOH) would be required to make 3 liters of a 0.10 molar sodium hydroxide solution?

Analogy Problem: How many ounces of lemonade powder would be required to make 3 quarts of lemonade of normal taste?

Gabel and Samuel found that when problems became complex, such as in dilution problems or in those involving the addition of solute to the original solution, students were unable to solve even the lemonade problems. For such problems, analogies would be useless unless teachers were willing to spend additional time teaching students how to use them. This could be time well spent.

Our objective, of course, is that students master concepts, not just proceed mechanically to the right answers. For straightforward molarity problems it appears that about 25 percent of students would be helped by the use of analogies. When analogies are used in instruction, however, they must be used consistently over a considerable period of time, and students must be helped to see the relationship between the analogy problem and the species problem. A. W. Friedel, Gabel, and Samuel (1988) found that, even after instruction using analogies over a two-week period, only about 50 percent of the class was able to match problems containing an analogy with the comparable chemistry problem!

Another practice that may promote concept development is that proposed by M. B. Rowe (1983). She advocates 2-minute pauses at 8- to 12-minute intervals in a science lecture. The pause gives students time to review what has been presented, fill in any gaps, and interpret the information for others, providing a solid foundation for the next portion of the lecture. Concept mapping (Novak, 1984, 1989) is one more technique to help students master and interrelate concepts. H. G. Elliott used a type of concept map in his 1982 research to explore misconceptions that affect problem solving. B. D. Goldman (1974) compared students who had prepared for chemistry with a special mathematics course stressing science applications with those who had taken a standard math course. The results were negative, but they may have been skewed, because about 50 percent of the students in the special course went on to take chemistry, while 95 percent of those in the standard math course did. M. P. Goodstein has prepared a set of materials (1983) outlining the mathematics necessary for physical science courses. A one-year preparatory course could be planned around Goodstein's materials.

A general heuristics approach might also improve students' problem-solving ability. In 1945, G. Poyla proposed four steps for problem solving in mathematics: understand the problem; devise a plan; carry out the plan; and look back over the process. A similar approach was specifically designed for chemistry problems by C. T. C. W. Mettes, A. Pilot, H. J. Roossink, and Kramers-Pals (1980). The schematic in Figure 2 summarizes their program of actions and methods. This structure has been used as a tool to determine how students approach chemistry problems. No data are available on its effectiveness in classroom use.

Bunce and H. Heikkinen (1986) compared students who used formal heuristics with those who did not. They asked beginning college chemistry students to complete a specially designed worksheet as they solved chemistry problems. The worksheet incorporated features of the information-processing model and included the following components:
- statement of the problem in words
- sketch if applicable
- recall of rules, definitions, etc.
- solution diagram
- mathematical solution
- review

The study showed no significant differences between students who used the worksheets and those who did not.

Several considerations may have affected this outcome, however. First, students found the worksheets time consuming and may not have used them consistently. Second, the students had already been taught to solve problems with the factor label method. Since they were not given extra time to think through the steps on the worksheet, students may well have returned to the factor label

Figure 2: *Principal Phases of Program of Actions and Methods*

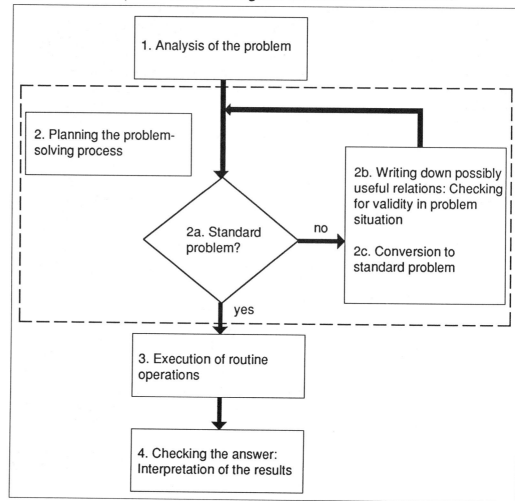

method as a crutch because it was quick, familiar, and produced satisfactory results under the time constraints of the test.

D. V. Frank and J. D. Herron reported a similar study in 1985. They provided information on problem solving to college students in an introductory chemistry course, using a three-step schema simpler than that of Bunce and Heikkinen: plan, solve, and review. Frank and Herron observed some student gains with this procedure.

Summary

Student difficulties with chemistry problems may result in part from the way problems are presented. Educators must take care to write problems that are clear and unambiguous, drawing on available information about the differences between expert and novice problem solving.

Experts rely on a body of well-linked concepts embedded in long-term memory. If students are going to develop into experts, much more time needs to be spent in the chemistry classroom determining their alternative conceptual frameworks and then providing qualitative instruction from a variety of contexts before introducing quantitative problems. Analogies, concept maps, and other techniques may help in this process.

Figure 3: *Problem solution using information processing model*

Problem: Find the volume occupied by 34 grams of ammonia at standard temperature and pressure.

Preliminary Redescription:

Given: Mass of NH_3 =   34 g
          Temperature   =   0°C
          Pressure   =   760 torr

Find: Volume of NH_3 in liters

Theoretical Redescription:

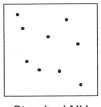

Standard NH_3
1 mole

# of particles   = 6.02×10^{23}
Pressure   =   760 torr
Temperature   =   0°C
Volume per mole   =   22.4 L/mole at 0°C and 760 torr
Mass per mole   =   14 g/mole N
                       + 3 x (1 g/mole H)
                  =   17 g/mole NH_3

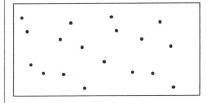

2 moles

$$\frac{34 \text{ g } NH_3}{17 \text{ g/mole}} = 2 \text{ moles } NH_3$$

2 moles has double the mass,
double the particles, and
double the volume, if temperature and
pressure remain constant.

Problem Solution:

$$\frac{34 \text{ g } NH_3}{17 \text{ g/mole}} = 2 \text{ moles } NH_3$$

2 moles NH_3 x 22.4 L/mole   = 44.8 L NH_3

Check on Reasonableness:

The mass is greater than the standard. In this case it is double. If the mass doubles, the number of particles must double and they must occupy double the space.
44.8 L is double the volume of the standard, 22.4 L.

Chemistry concept development can begin in the elementary and junior high classroom. The present trend is to postpone basic facts and concepts such as mass, volume, heat, and temperature until the upper elementary and junior high levels.

Research reveals a strong link between problem-solving and proportional reasoning. Other aptitudes also affect students' success. Teachers who are aware of these findings might set different levels of expectation for different students. For students with low scores in proportional reasoning, it may be valuable to stress concept development rather than problem solving.

Directions for Further Research

Although much more research needs to be done, the information-processing model of cognitive psychology (Reif, 1983) offers promise for helping students to solve chemistry problems. This model incorporates many of the features discussed in the present review. According to this view, in order to become an expert problem solver, one needs to master a body of basic concepts, to link those concepts into a conceptual framework, and to be able to retrieve them from long-term memory. As one approaches a problem, one must first make a basic redescription and then a theoretical redescription using stored concepts. Once the problem is redescribed and restructured in terms of a person's own conceptual framework, he or she will need to consider alternative pathways, construct a solution, and assess its reasonableness. Figure 3 illustrates this method as applied to a chemistry problem.

How could this model alter the teaching of chemistry? It suggests, first, that if concepts are to be learned more thoroughly, less will have to be attempted in the curriculum. It means that students will have to be taught to represent matter on three levels: the physical or macroscopic level, the symbolic level (as in formulas), and the particulate or microscopic level. Then, students will be able to redescribe or restructure each new problem. It may also suggest that they not be given algorithms or crutches like the factor label method, which encourage students to obtain answers without having to think through their implications.

And where might these new methods lead? We hope that they will lead to chemistry students solving problems more intelligently, being able to solve complex problems of types they haven't practiced, enjoying chemistry, and feeling that what they are learning fits together and makes sense. Science education researchers do not promise a panacea for all students, but they do continue to seek out what can be done to improve chemistry problem-solving achievement.

References

Albert, E. (1978). Development of the concept of heat in children. *Science Education, 62,* 389–399.

Ben-Zvi, R., Eylon, B., and Silberstein, J. (1982, April). *Student conception of gas and solid difficulties to function in a multi-atomic context, part II.* Paper presented at the National Association of Research in Science Teaching Conference, Lake Geneva, WI.

Brenner, M. E. (March, 1989). *Everyday problem solving: Dollar wise, penny foolish.* Paper presented at the National Association of Research in Science Teaching Conference, San Francisco.

Bunce, D. M., and Gabel, D. L. (1989, April). *Using categorizations to enhance chemistry problem-solving skills.* Paper presented at the National Association of Research in Science Teaching Conference, San Francisco.

Bunce, D. M., and Heikkinen, H. (1986). The effects of an explicit problem-solving approach on mathematical chemistry achievement. *Journal of Research in Science Teaching, 23,* 11–20.

Carter, C. S., LaRussa, A., and Bodner, G. M. (1985, April). *Spatial ability in general chemistry.* Paper presented at the National Association for Research in Science Teaching Conference, French Lick Springs, IN.

Cassels, J. R. T., and Johnstone, A. H. (1984). The effect of language on student performance on multiple-choice tests in chemistry. *Journal of Chemical Education, 61,* 613-615.

Cassels, J. R. T., and Johnstone, A. H. (1985, January). *Words that matter in science.* (Report available from Education Division, the Royal Society of Chemistry, Burlington House, Piccadilly, London W1V 0BN).

Cervellati, R., Montuschi, A., Perugini, D., Grimellini-Tomasini, N., and Balandi, B. P. (1982). Investigation of secondary school students' understanding of the mole concept in Italy. *Journal of Chemical Education, 59,* 852-856.

Champagne, A. B., Klopfer, L. E., and Chaiklin, S. (1984, April). *The ubiquitous quantities.* Paper presented at the annual meeting of the American Educational Research Association, New Orleans.

De Vos, W., and Verdonk, A. H. (1987). A new road to reaction, part 4: The substance and its molecules. *Journal of Chemical Education, 64,* 692-694.

Duncan, I. M., and Johnstone, A. H. (1973). The mole concept. *Educational Chemistry, 10,* 212-214.

Elliott, H. G. (1982). Links and nodes in problem-solving. *Journal of Chemical Education, 59,* 719-720.

Enochs, L. G., and Gabel, D. L. (1984). Preservice elementary teachers' conceptions of volume. *School Science and Mathematics, 84,* 670-679.

Erickson, G. L. (1979). Children's conceptions of heat and temperature. *Science Education, 63,* 221-230.

Erickson, G. L. (1980). Children's viewpoints of heat: A second look. *Science Education, 64,* 323-336.

Eylon, B., Ben-Zvi, R., and Silberstein, J. (1982, April). *Student conception of gas and solid difficulties to function in a multi-atomic context, part I.* Paper presented to the National Association for Research in Science Teaching Conference, Lake Geneva, WI.

Falls, T. H., and Voss, B. (1985, April). *The ability of high school chemistry students to solve computational problems requiring proportional reasoning as affected by item in-task variables.* Paper presented at the National Association for Research in Science Teaching Conference, French Lick Springs, IN.

Frank, D. V., and Herron, J. D. (1985, April). *The effect of a problem-solving teaching method on student problem-solving processes.* Paper presented at the National Association for Research in Science Teaching Conference, French Lick Springs, IN.

Friedel, A. W., Gabel, D. L., and Samuel, K. V. (1988). *Using analogs for meaningful chemistry problem solving: Does it increase understanding?* Manuscript submitted for publication.

Gabel, D. L. (1981). *Facilitating problem solving in high school chemistry.* Bloomington, IN: Indiana University, School of Education. (ERIC Document Reproduction Service No. ED 210 192)

Gabel, D. L., Hunn, D., and Samuel, K. V. (1987). Understanding the particulate nature of matter. *Journal of Chemical Education, 64,* 695-697.

Gabel, D. L., and Samuel, K. V. (1986). High school students' ability to solve molarity problems and their analog counterparts. *Journal of Research in Science Teaching, 23,* 83-94.

Gabel, D. L., and Sherwood, R. D. (1983). Facilitating problem solving in high school chemistry. *Journal of Research in Science Teaching, 20,* 163-177.

Gabel, D. L., and Sherwood, R. D. (1984). Analyzing difficulties with mole-concept tasks by using familiar analog tasks. *Journal of Research in Science Teaching, 21,* 843-851.

Gabel, D. L., Sherwood, R. D., and Enochs, L. G. (1984). Problem-solving skills of high school chemistry students. *Journal of Research in Science Teaching, 21,* 221-233.

Goldman, B. D. (1974). The effects of an experimental mathematics curriculum stressing problem-solving skills in science on student achievement in chemistry. *Dissertation Abstracts International, 35,* 166A.

Goodstein, M. P. (1983). *Applications in proportional problem solving.* Menlo Park, CA: Addison Wesley.

Gower, D. M., Daniels, J. J., and Lloyd, G. (1977a). Hierarchies among the concepts which underlie the mole. *School Science Review, 59,* 285-299.

Gower, D. M., Daniels, D. J., and Lloyd, G. (1977b). The mole concept. *School Science Review, 58,* 658-676.

Greenbowe, T. J. (1983). An investigation of variables involved in chemistry problem solving *Dissertation Abstracts International, 44,* 3651A.

Griffiths, A. K., Kass, H., and Cornish, A. G. (1983). Validation of a learning hierarchy for the mole concept. *Journal of Research in Science Teaching, 20,* 639-654.

Hayes, J. R. (1981). *The complete problem solver.* Philadelphia: The Franklin Institute.

Johnstone, A. H. (1983). Chemical education research, facts, findings, and consequences. *Journal of Chemical Education, 60,* 968–971.

Kramers-Pals, H., Lambrechts, J., and Wolff, P. J. (1982). Recurrent difficulties: Solving quantitative problems. *Journal of Chemical Education, 59,* 509–513.

Mayer, R. E. (1982).The psychology of mathematical problem solving. In F.K. Lester and J. Garofalo (Eds.), *Mathematical problem solving: Issues in research* (pp. 1–11). Philadelphia: Franklin Institute.

Mettes, C. T. C. W., Pilot, A., Roossink, H. J., and Kramers-Pals, H. (1980). Teaching and learning problem solving in science. *Journal of Chemical Education, 57,* 882–885.

Novak, J. D. (1984). Application of advances in learning theory and philosophy of science to the improvement of chemistry teaching. *Journal of Chemical Education, 61,* 607–612.

Novak, J. D. (1989). The role of content and process in the education of science teachers. In P. F. Brandwein and A. H. Passow (Eds.), *Gifted young in science: Potential through performance* (pp.307–320). Washington, DC: NSTA.

Novick, S., and Menis, J. (1976). A study of student perceptions of the mole concept. *Journal of Chemical Education, 61,* 720–722.

Novick, S., and Nussbaum, J. (1978). Junior high school pupils' understanding of the particulate nature of matter: An interview study. *Science Education, 62,* 273–281.

Novick, S., and Nussbaum, J. (1981). Pupils' understanding of the particulate nature of matter: A cross-age study. *Science Education, 65,* 187–196.

Nurrenbern, S. C. (1979). *Problem-solving behaviors of concrete and formal operational high school chemistry students when solving chemistry problems requiring Piagetian formal reasoning skills.* Unpublished doctoral dissertation, Purdue University, Lafayette, IN.

Osborne, R. J., and Cosgrove, M. M. (1983). Children's conceptions of the changes of state of water. *Journal of Research in Science Teaching, 20,* 825–838.

Poyla, G. (1945). *How to solve it.* Princeton, NJ: Princeton University Press.

Reif, F. (1983). How can chemists teach problem solving? *Journal of Chemical Education, 60,* 948–953.

Rowe, M. B. (1983). Getting chemistry off the killer course list. *Journal of Chemical Education, 60,* 954–956.

Shayer, M., and Wylam, H. (1981). The development of the concepts of heat and temperature in 10–13 year olds. *Journal of Research in Science Teaching, 18,* 419–434.

Shepherd, D. L., and Renner, J. W. (1982). Student understandings and misunderstandings of states of matter and density changes. *School Science and Mathematics, 82,* 650–665.

Squires, F. H. (1977). An analysis of sex differences and cognitive styles on science problem-solving situations. *Dissertation Abstracts International, 38,* 2688A.

Ward, C. R., and Herron, J. D. (1980). Helping students understand formal chemical concepts. *Journal of Research in Science Teaching, 17,* 387–400.

Wheeler, A. E., and Kass, H. (1977, March). *Proportional reasoning in introductory high school chemistry.* Paper presented at the annual meeting of the National Association for Research in Science Teaching, Cincinnati, OH.

Williams, H., Turner, C. W., Debreuil, L., Fast, J., and Berestiansky, J. (1979). Formal operational reasoning by chemistry students. *Journal of Chemical Education, 56,* 599–600.

Yarroch, W. L. (1985). Student understanding of chemical equation balancing. *Journal of Research in Science Teaching, 22,* 449–459.

Problem Solving in Practice

Donald Robert Woods
McMaster University
Hamilton, Ontario
Canada

Many equate the teaching of problem solving with blackboard demonstrations and the assignment of homework problems. But research has shown this approach to be one of the *least* effective methods of developing problem-solving skills (Woods, Crowe, Hoffman, and Wright, 1979 and 1985; Caillot, 1983), which are among our most advanced mental skills, corresponding to the higher levels in B. S. Bloom's cognitive taxonomy. We teachers can do much more for our students than simply say, "Try solving these problems," or "Watch me while I write out this well-polished script of the highlights of the problem-solving process." What research has shown is that we can define problem solving and identify its cognitive and attitudinal components.

Students come to us with many misconceptions about problem solving, however, and with bad habits that students persist in using to approach problems. Students have been doing *exercises* for years and are generally quite good at it; along with their teachers, they have been calling this *problem solving.* Similarly, we teachers have been "working examples" on the board for years, and we think we're good at explaining and modeling the problem-solving process. In reality, it is only when we get stuck and feel panic at not knowing how to solve a problem that we really start to employ the skills this book addresses. When we use these important skills intuitively, we tend to dismiss them as "just experience."

The most challenging task in problem solving is to create a representation of the problem situation. Some call this "exploring the situation"; others describe it as making connections between the problem situation and the subject's background experience. Whatever it is called, each person approaches it uniquely. Knowledge and problem solving are intimately connected: How we learn affects how we retrieve ideas and how we create representations.

Knowledge about the principles and laws of biology, chemistry, physics, and the Earth sciences is not sufficient. Each discipline also has specific tacit information from experience. This kind of information is difficult to extract from our own experience, let alone communicate to our students. Yet students *need* it for effective problem solving.

To develop problem solving skills, a teacher needs to assume the role of facilitator and coach, rather than lecturer and provider of information.

Establishing Educational Goals

Just as we set content-learning objectives for our science courses, so we should set skill goals for problem solving or mental processing. These aims enable us to design a teaching/learning environment that promotes problem solving, gives

Table 1A: *One Example of General Learning Objectives**

To become aware of the process whereby you solve problems.
To be able to describe verbally the process whereby you solve problems.
To be able to write out the process whereby you solve problems.
To be able to state the steps and substeps in a strategy to solve problems; state the relationship among analysis, creativity, decision making, and generalization, and the steps and substeps; state the characteristics by which we classify different types of problems; state the relationship between the type of problem to be solved and the steps in the strategy; state the prerequisites.
Given a textbook problem statement, to be able to identify correctly the unknown or goal.
Given a textbook problem statement, to be able to draw a "good" diagram.
Given a drawing or sketch pertinent to the problem, to be able to identify correctly the system consistent with the information given.
Given a textbook problem statement, to be able to identify the stated constraints and to list reasonable inferred constraints.
Given a textbook problem statement, to be able to identify the assumptions and simplifications to be made.
Given a textbook problem statement, to be able to identify key trigger words that relate to the assumptions or background fundamentals.
Given a problem-solving situation where you are stuck, to be able to identify where you are, where you want to go, and the obstacles that are hindering you.
To develop the skill necessary to complete the remaining steps of the strategy
    to create, analyze, generalize, and simplify
    to manage resources
    to see structure in knowledge
    to develop a cognitive base
    to identify personal preference
    to be able to shift the data base
    to learn heuristics and develop personal skill at applying them
    to learn quantitative techniques and develop skill at applying them . . . .
Given a real, non-textbook problem, to be able to define the real problem to be solved.
Given a problem . . . , to recall the stated problem-solving strategy and elements and supply these to solve the problem . . . .
Given a situation where it is not evident that a problem-solving strategy is required, identify when the strategy and elements should be applied, then show comprehension . . . .
To analyze what you do when you apply the given strategy and identify personal preferences about steps and elements.
To develop your own strategy for solving problems.
To develop an ability to solve problems effectively as a member of a group.

*Table 1A based on an earlier version that was published in the *Journal of College Science Teaching, 13*(4), 320–321, Washington, DC: NSTA, 1984, February.

Table 1B: *One Example of Detailed Learning Objectives for Decision Making**

Given a situation, you will be able to decide if a decision is within your control or not.

Given a decision statement, you will be able to convert it into a *results* statement.

Given a situation, you will be able to list the steps in the decision-making process.

Given a situation and a decision to be made, you will be able to identify whether individual or group process might be more appropriate.

Given a decision, you will be able to state whether it is a decision under certainty, risk, uncertainty, or conflict.

Given a decision that you judged to be under certainty, you will be able to list the measurable criteria, assign weightings, and rate or rank each option in order to demonstrate the decision matrix procedure and select the best option. . . .

Given a decision that you judged to be under risk, you will be able to identify pertinent "states of nature," and estimate the probability for each, using "decision trees" or "tables" in the process.

*From a chemical engineering course at McMaster University

students an overview of the program and what is expected of them, and helps us to prepare effective evaluation materials.

Twenty years ago it would have been very difficult to delineate goals in problem solving. Now, many models are available. V. Gold, M. J. Kershaw, and D. J. Millen (1980) and L. Harrisberger, R. Heydinger, J. Seeley, and M. Talburtt (1976) list some broad, general goals in the areas of chemistry and engineering, respectively. L. Burton (1979) identifies procedural and component skills for mathematics. H. S. Barrows and R. M. Tamblyn (1980) have developed for clinical medical skills learning objectives that are relevant for problem solving. K. O'Brien and A. Doherty (1979) list six competency levels for each of five areas: communication, analysis, problem solving, the making of value judgments, and interpersonal interactions. D. R. Woods (1979b) lists 18 sequential skills, with detail-levels of achievement for each. Finally, P. Smith (1981) gives an extensive, structured taxonomy. The teacher's task is to use these groups of goals to create learning objectives for developing problem-solving skills in a specific course and to incorporate them into the course description.

Once the activities are identified, resources can be surveyed, learning activities chosen, and evaluation procedures selected. M. Knowles (1975) and Woods (1983a) give a general overview of ways to add problem-solving components to any course.

Cognitive Research and the Science Classroom

Cognitive, educational, and attitudinal psychology provide the basic data, as well as some practical suggestions for improving problem solving. The fundamentals are still being explored, but we can identify some patterns:

- We know a bit about how the brain functions, about the relationships between short- and long-term memory, for example (see Entwistle, 1981).
- We act to satisfy needs; Maslow's model is acceptable, although some of his specific assertions are disputed.
- We function best if we have a target or goal.
- We should concentrate on situations over which we have control.
- We may criticize a person's ideas and performance but *not* the person.
- We should search for something positive in every situation; however,
- We should not neglect the negative complement to any situation (Wason and Johnson-Laird, 1972).
- We can use pencil and paper to extend the limited capacity of short-term memory.
- We should address both attitudinal and cognitive components.

We must be attentive to ongoing research and all its implications for our programs.

Overviews

Four reviews of research on problem solving drew similar conclusions. J. F. Voss reviewed the literature on cognitive psychology to 1985 to arrive at some characteristics of effective problem solving in practice. Competent problem solvers, Voss writes,

- possess a *knowledge structure* for the subject of their expertise
  1. arranged hierarchically, with key words and pointers (surface structures) at the lower levels, and fundamental laws and principles at the higher levels
  2. including procedural knowledge, remembered experiences, and acquired skills
  3. open to continual modification by new information and new experiences
- know how to create a *visual representation,* to reconstruct a situation qualitatively (novices tend to combine familiar equations)
- acknowledge that "creating the internal representation" of the problem is the most challenging and crucial task
- know how to "chunk" information
- approach *problems* with a working-backward strategy; *exercises* by working forward
- monitor, summarize, reason, and evaluate as they progress through the problem-solving process (novices, lacking this skill, tend to confuse related issues and subproblems with solutions)

Voss suggests that ample evidence is available to show that teachers can teach effective, domain-specific skills in problem solving.

The anonymous mathematics educators who published "The Problem of Problem Solving" in 1982 provide a second review as they agree on some implications for the teaching of problem solving. For instance, although there are no magic formulas for teaching or learning problem solving, it can be taught, at least within a specific discipline. (Researchers disagree on whether general problem-solving skills applicable to all areas can be identified.) Further, developmental level affects problem-solving ability. And, while students share some common misconceptions about problem solving, just as they do about some science subjects, these misconceptions can be anticipated and remedied. Finally, some heuristics are more useful than others, but there is no optimal heuristic for all situations, even within a domain. Therefore, teachers should

- use a variety of heuristics and one overall process, such as G. Polya's four-step strategy
- encourage students to solve different problems with the same heuristic and also, to apply different heuristics to the same problem

- provide many and varied problems
- help students to display the mental processes they use when they solve problems
- offer ample time for reflection on the process and help students to generalize and see similarities across problems
- expect students to estimate answers and to test the reasonableness of answers
- encourage students to look back after they have reached a solution

A third review by R. Glaser (1984) addresses the relationship between problem solving, knowledge structures, and how we might teach these concepts. Glaser asks whether we teach awareness of the processes used when we solve problems; whether we teach problem solving as a general skill (as in a separate course based on everyday problem situations); whether we teach problem-solving heuristics in the context of a subject such as biology (an approach which can be so specific that it can lack carry-over to other situations); and whether we teach reasoning integrated smoothly into a subject. Glaser suggests that none of these approaches adequately accounts for the key importance that knowledge structure has on problem solving. Voss' conclusions, summarized above, concur; so do those of M. M. Waldrop (1984).

The fourth review by L. B. Greenfield (1979, 1980) summarizes research and surveys various programs for teaching problem solving. She highlights the work of A. Whimbey, J. K. Stonewater, J. Lochhead and J. Clement, Woods and his colleagues, Bloom and L. J. Broder, and J. H. Larkin and F. Reif. Experts, these thinkers agree, tend to redescribe problem situations qualitatively; novices try to combine equations. Further, the researchers find that

- a strategy for solving problems is available and effective
- teachers can describe their own problem-solving processes but have difficulty specifying which ones their students should use
- the characteristics of good problem solvers can be listed
- students in science tend to be formula centered and have misconceptions about both subject domains and problem solving
- emphasis should be placed on the process students use to solve problems and not just their answers
- teachers should help students to organize their knowledge qualitatively to "chunk" relationships

Establishing the Knowledge Base

Research helps us to understand learning and its implications for science educators. Knowledge to be gained usually takes several forms. It can be composed of fundamental, subject-specific principles such as those in textbooks—for example, the conservation of mass. Or it can be tacit general information about the subject. (This information does not usually appear in textbooks, although experts in the discipline are familiar with it. However, often unaware of the knowledge acquired by experience, they frequently cannot transmit it. Many researchers are trying to identify or develop methods for sharing such information.) A third type of knowledge is episodic, specific information based on personal experience. A fourth, is procedural—knowledge of what to do in various types of situations. Finally, knowledge can take the form of skill at problem solving, communicating, evaluating, interacting with other individuals, working in groups, and learning how to learn.

Students' learning of fundamental principles often meets resistance from their ingrained misconceptions. Subject-specific misconceptions are described in several of the papers in this volume, particularly in those on Earth science, physics, genetics, and chemistry. Much work has been done to identify the misconceptions many students have about the fundamentals of science. Some misconceptions in physics have been researched by D. F. Trowbridge and L. C.

McDermott (1980, December; 1981, March), H. Helm (1980), Lochhead and Clement (1979), and many others, including R. M. Snider in this volume. Though there has not been a great deal of work done in studying misconceptions in biology, M. U. Smith and R. Good (1984) and K. M. Fisher, J. I. Lipson, A. C. Hildebrand, L. Miguel, N. Schoenberg, and N. Porter (1986, February) provide some data. Further, earlier in this volume, Smith summarizes such problems in genetics, C. R. Ault, Jr., treats them in Earth science, and D. L. Gabel discusses them in chemistry. See also Woods (1983c, September/October). Larkin (1982) has completed a significant study to identify topics that are "difficult" to learn in the area of mechanics; to extend their range, his findings await teachers' anecdotal evidence and further research. Many have suggested the importance of learning "pointers" to help learners relate the concepts in the problem situation to the knowledge structure. R. Bhaskar and H. Simon (1970) provide examples.

Reif (1982a) and Larkin et al (1980) have emphasized the importance of elusive tacit information. Although I describe some initial efforts to identify such knowledge in engineering (1983b), little research seems available on the subject in the "pure" sciences. Some suggest that problem solving be classed as procedural knowledge. I prefer to consider problem solving as a subject domain in itself like biology and chemistry.

Different forms of knowledge are linked by structures. How can teachers help students to create knowledge structures? We know we want students to think qualitatively and in terms of observable behaviors, and we want students to hook new knowledge onto existing structures. Is this an easy task? Do all students use the same tactics to create these structures? Much has been learned about how students learn. N. Entwistle's is probably the most comprehensive review (1981). He does a superb job of assimilating the many different perspectives: general evidence about how students learn, data from cognitive psychology, the attitudinal components of learning, and the role of personality. College students differ in their views of the university and their role in the learning process, in their attitudes and fears, and in their learning styles. Entwistle names six different learning styles: deep versatile, comprehensive (A), operational (B), surface, hard work, and drop out.

This analysis of learning styles looks into those elements in a given body of information on which students choose to focus and what effort they expend to relate the new information to previous information. Some students focus on the overview, some on the details. Some relate new information to episodic information they already possess, and some do not. Ideally, we would all want to use and have our students use what Entwistle calls a "deep-versatile" (A and B) style. He describes Heath's finding that most first-year college students tend to be comprehensive (A) or operational (B) types, but that most college graduates over time develop the combined A and B style. Entwistle also reports that Marton found that he could not classify students by any particular set of styles. The style of learning depends upon the situation. For example, "deep processors" will switch to being "surface processors" when they have too much work to do, when they become anxious, when they anticipate test questions that require surface processing, and when they perceive the department or the instructor as rewarding surface performance. Thus, even a student who has mastered the desirable A and B learning style will adopt a less desirable style when the learning environment seems to call for it. This research suggests that creating knowledge structures isn't easy and illustrates some factors that influence their development.

I suggest to students who want to develop useful learning structures the following general principles:
• Put yourself in control. No one else can be responsible for what you learn: It is your life and your learning.

Table 2: *Research in Summary of Learning Styles from Educational Psychology**

Student's View of the Purpose of a University & His/Her Role	Student's Attitudes and Fears	Learning Styles Characteristics		Comment	Name or Style of Learning
		At the start of a learning task	Later in the learning task		
University has personal meaning. [It] suppl[ies] resources; I learn	Autonomous, self-learner	Get overview	Relate to personal experience via analogies but identify limitations and detailed analysis of evidence tied to the overall conclusions	Depth understanding	Deep versatile (combined A and B)
		(a) Get an overview	(b) Reorganize to relate to personal experience and understanding	Incomplete understanding because of inappropriate analogies to experience	Comprehensive A
[Authorities] tell me "what," and I reproduce it.	I'm afraid of failing; therefore, I study hard. I study what is in the syllabus.	(c) Detailed analysis of evidence	(d) Which I relate to get an overview	Incomplete understanding because does not use analogies or experience to help	Operational B
		Memorize everything	Overlearn	Surface or memorized ideas with no relationships	Surface Underdeveloped
I want good grades, high marks	I hope for success; I'm confident, I'm stable	Any of the above schemes	Any of the above schemes	High grades with or without understanding	Hard worker. "E" for effort
Social life is great.					Drop out

* Table 2 based on work of N. Entwistle. First published in the *Journal of College Science Teaching, 14*(5), 445, Washington, DC: NSTA, 1985, March/April.

● Make written notes about what you are studying. Do not passively underline or highlight. Be active. Rephrase the ideas in your own words.
● Identify global perspectives on the subject. Write out your own advance organizers to give yourself the big picture.
● Use any of the many techniques which can help you to see the structure in the subject and to identify the key facts and concepts. For instance, try
    1. Beetle diagrams, mind maps, or concept maps to show the interrelationships among the topics (Buzan, 1974; Novak, 1984, 1989; Woods, 1984b)

2. Larkin's checklist for identifying the key components in any concept (1975; Woods, 1984a)

3. visual display networks (Ashmore et al, 1979)

4. the Gowin Vee, or Lewis' postulate structure (Novak and Gowin, 1984; Novak, 1989; Lewis, 1982)

5. Clement's interaction diagrams (1978a) to show the effect of variables on behavior; also his analysis of the various levels of abstraction that interact in our knowledge structure

6. Reif's "concept scripts," in which learners create statements such as the following for each concept: Apply [some general principle or definition] to [some particular entity] at [some particular time or during some particular time interval] with [some particular description] (Reif et al, 1976; Reif, 1982a; Reif and Heller, 1982)

7. key relations diagrams or memory boards created to summarize the knowledge components (see Mettes et al, 1980; and Woods, Wright, Hoffman, Swartman, and Doig, 1975)

- Extract the experience factors from the subject (see Woods, 1984b).
- Try to relate the new information to past episodic experiences.

Effective and Ineffective Problem Solvers (Experts Versus Novices)

Most of the research in this area has focused on college students. H. S. Lin (1979a, 1979b) used personal interviews and protocol analysis to study and document the problem-solving difficulties encountered by successive classes of freshman physics students at the Massachusetts Institute of Technology. Bloom and L. J. Broder (1950) studied the problem-solving difficulties of university students in science and other fields. With an emphasis on learning concepts and the difficulty students subsequently had recalling ideas, Larkin (1979a, 1979b, 1980), Larkin et al (1980), and Reif et al (1976) studied novices and experts solving problems in first-year physics. Larkin (1982) also compared the process sequences used by a computer programmed to solve physics mechanics problems with the sequences chosen by students. Other work contrasted novices and experts solving manometer problems in physics in which spatial images of the levels of liquids and the configuration of the manometer tube might be important. Lochhead and Clement (1979) observed first-year engineering students solving problems in freshman physics. Their results, obtained partly by the Whimbey-pair method and partly by protocol analysis, describe general thinking difficulties and difficulties with the content of physics. M. T. H. Chi et al (1981) also reported results in the area of physics. M. Selvaratnam (1983), Larkin (1983), and R. J. Freeland and Larkin (1984) document the difficulties students have in solving problems in the context of chemistry.

In the McMaster project, professors became students again through the full four-year undergraduate engineering program, attending classes and observing a group of volunteers as they solved their ordinary homework assignments. Each student's performance on typical freshman-to-senior-level problems was compared to an expert's performance, to that of representative undergraduate humanities and engineering students at two other universities, to that of graduate students, to that of sophomore physics students, and to that of applicants to medical school (Woods, Wright, Hoffman, Swartman, and Doig, 1975; Woods, Crowe, Hoffman, and Wright, 1979; Woods and Crowe, 1984; Woods, 1987). Smith (1988) and Smith and Good (1984) contrast experts' and novices' abilities in the context of biology.

Whimbey (1975) contrasted effective and ineffective problem solvers on IQ problems. A. H. Schoenfeld (1979a, 1979b, 1979c), and Schoenfeld and D. J. Herrmann (1981) focused on the differences between novices and experts on

Table 3: *Differences Between Problem-Solving Styles of Novices and Experts**

Novices or persons needing improvement	Experts or experienced problem solvers
Emphasize speed, recall past experiences, and assume that these apply precisely to the situation at hand.	Emphasize care and precision, see each situation afresh with fair exploration of alternatives, and doublecheck.
Unaware of mental process used when solving problems.	Aware of process and use well-developed, explicit mental activities to bring care, diversity, and completeness to the issues, hypotheses, and alternatives considered.
Confuse and mix different stages of the problem-solving process. Unaware of this problem and so do not apply an organized plan of attack or strategy.	Consider the problem by stages, identifying a time for problem definition, exploration and assessment, planning, implementation . . . evaluation, checking back, or similar mental activities.
Fail to know the meanings of all the words in the problem situation.	Refresh their memory about meanings of all words in the problem situation and seek clarification where ambiguity exists.
Jump into problem, quickly limit the initial problem statement, and select a first-impression solution without adequately defining or exploring the problem situation. Haste is later manifest when the wrong problem is solved, in heated justification of initial incorrect judgments, or in blind fixation.	Identify from the initial problem statement that a problem does indeed exist over which they have control, by defining constraints and criteria; exploring issues or pertinent variables, or factors that impinge; . . . seeing short and long time scale implications, and carefully keeping options open before formulating precisely.
Tend to make decisions based on given information and past experiences. Fail to address openly the question of new information needed or dismiss the problem completely as "impossible to solve" because of insufficient knowledge.	Identify necessary information.
Confuse issues, constraints, criteria, possible solutions, and procedures.	Differentiate clearly issues, constraints, criteria, possible solutions, and procedures.
Choose an issue, possible solution, or procedure without consciously exploring numerous alternatives.	Generate (usually in a "deferred-judgment" atmosphere) many practical and perhaps impractical alternative issues, solutions, procedures, means, cause-effect relationships, and/or consequences when pertinent in the overall strategy. (Usually not satisfied by 50 alternative ideas.)
Make decisions without an identified, measurable criterion.	Establish measurable criterion and apply when deciding.
Are unable to get themselves "unstuck."	Have set of heuristics to help them get "unstuck."
Are unclear on evaluative procedures and unable to accurately assess own problem-solving skills.	Have clear set of objectives and can accurately use these to assess progress and personal strengths and weaknesses.
Classify problem type as being "similar" based on the wording of the situation. . . .	Classify problem type as being similar based on fundamental principles and underlying cause-effect relationships.

*Table 3 based on an earlier version that was published in the *Journal of College Science Teaching, 13*(2), 112–113, Washington, DC: NSTA, 1983, November.

college-level math problems. P. P. Heppner et al (1982) contrasted the attitudes of effective versus ineffective problem solvers. From this wealth of data, we can identify traits that are independent of subject domain. I have summarized some of the details in "PS Corner," 1988–1989. Some of the commonly observed difficulties students have in solving problems and some contrasts between different problem-solving approaches are summarized in Table 3. The top 10 percent of our students seem to be able to cope no matter what we do in the classroom, so these observations of unsuccessful styles apply to the majority of the students—the other 90 percent.

Personal Style

Each individual has his or her personal style of interacting with information. The importance of this style varies depending on which step of the problem-solving process we are performing. At step one, "Read the problem statement and identify the stated problem," personal style seems to play a small role. At the crucial next step, "Explore the situation and create a representation of the problem," personal style seems to play a major role, and each person performs differently.

Similarly, personal style affects the ease with which we discover and assimilate new information. Research is beginning to provide indications that might guide us in teaching different types of students. An analysis of three kinds of approaches—that of the visualizer, the verbalizer, and the symbolizer—has helped students modify the ways they assimilate information, select textbooks, and think about problem situations. A visualizer prefers diagrams, sketches, and graphs; a verbalizer is comfortable with word descriptions; and a symbolizer likes to work with symbols and equations. Although instruments to measure these dimensions are being developed, the measures are as yet not validated and the impact of the differing approaches is as yet not measured (Woods, 1984b).

The Myers-Briggs type indicator (MBTI) and the Kolb learning-style indicator have been used to help students and instructors identify ways to facilitate learning (McCaulley et al, 1983; Sloan and Jens, 1982; Sloan, 1982). In these cases, the instrument has been developed and validated, but the implications of what it measures have yet to be elucidated. C. F. Yokomoto and J. R. Ware reported in 1982 their experiences using the Sensing versus Intuitive dimension of the MBTI to select students for sections of classes and to choose the manner of presenting information. R. J. Yinger (1980) suggests that personal preference affects the style we use in asking questions and seeking information.

The best known developmental measures are W. G. Perry, Jr.'s, scales of attitudinal development (1970) and J. Piaget's concepts about concrete and formal stages. Details of how to use Perry's ideas in the classroom are given by P. Fitch and R. S. Culver (1984) and Culver (1987). The Piagetian levels seem pertinent for high school students, who are generally in the process of shifting from one stage to another. R. Karplus and colleagues (1977) have developed excellent resource materials to help us appreciate the significance of Piaget's ideas for our teaching of science.

General Implications for Teaching Problem Solving

Research on the psychological foundations of problem solving, the way the knowledge structure is built, the difficulties students have with solving problems, and the impact of personal characteristics, including developmental level, lead to some overall conclusions on how to best teach problem solving. First, we should resist the temptation to use the latest "how to do it" book. Rather, we should rely on the fundamental findings of cognitive and behavioral research to guide in the selection of materials and approaches.

Evidence from research gives us guidelines for helping students to create knowledge structures or, as I interpret this activity, to work at the "comprehen-

sion" level of Bloom's Taxonomy. Students must be able to
- think quantitatively and qualitatively (Clement, 1978a; Eylon and Reif, 1984; and Reif, 1982b)
- know the *what* and *why* of each concept, and *when* to apply it (Larkin et al, 1980)
- relate new information to past experience (Entwistle found this trait characteristic of deep-versatile learners)
- describe the organizational structure into which the new knowledge fits and express the new knowledge in terms of principles and abstract fundamental postulates (Glaser, 1984; Novak and Gowin, 1984; Voss, 1985)
- express the new knowledge at all four of Clement's levels: practical knowledge, qualitative models, concrete mathematical knowledge and symbols, and mathematical manipulation (Clement, 1978a, 1978b)
- identify the "pointers" that relate the knowledge to everyday descriptions (Eylon and Reif, 1984)
- "chunk" the knowledge into collections or systems

The surprising thing about this list is that at first glance these behaviors seem to bear no direct relationship to problem solving. They are strategies to facilitate learning in general. But problem-solving research makes it clear that learning is vital to effective problem solving. So teachers should consider using a problem-based approach to learning.

Having helped students use these approaches in so far as possible, next make your own tacit information explicit and share it with your students. Try to explain why you, as a chemist, know a certain reaction is improbable; why, as a biologist, you find a certain answer reasonable. At McMaster University, we require engineering students to memorize numerical, order-of-magnitude values for all the phenomena with which we deal routinely and then to apply those values. For example: Is 50 kJ/mol a "reasonable" heat of reaction? If I punched you in the nose with a force of 5 N, would it hurt? J. Ogborn (1977) and P. J. Black (1980) give a good introduction to how tacit information might be made explicit for physicists. D. Boud and T. G. F. Gray (1978) list examples in the context of engineering, and H. H. Friedman (1987) provides models for medicine.

Problem solving is a subject, just like chemistry and the Earth sciences. It is an evolving domain with its own fundamentals, its own typical misconceptions (see Woods, 1984a), and its own specific concepts, which include the mathematics of decision making, our knowledge of organizational behavior, and the characteristics of effective groups. But it is difficult to think about the concepts that make up the domain, let alone describe them, display them, and develop in others the ability to apply them. After 20 years in the field, I still find neither the terminology nor the concepts easy.

Problem solving is a domain in which attitudinal components matter a great deal: Anxiety, ability to cope with ambiguity, and motivation count, for example. Problem solving also interacts more than any other domain with the subject matter of other fields and the knowledge structures they contain. Problem solving comes into play whenever we try to attain the highest levels of Bloom's Taxonomy in any subject, be it English, history, physics, or mathematics. And as E. P. Torrance (1979), Larkin (1980), and Voss (1985) all maintain, there are no shortcuts; problem solving, which requires patience and perseverance, is intrinsically difficult to teach.

I believe the main educational challenge is to develop students' confidence that they can solve problems in a given discipline and apply the same skills to problems in other areas. A laboratory notebook can be useful for self-evaluation of performance and to hold records of three kinds: the knowledge gained through problem-solving workshops; the weekly application of that knowledge to homework assignments in one class other than the problem-solving course; and the use of the same knowledge to solve everyday problems (Woods, Crowe, Taylor, and Wood, 1984). This approach combines the techniques suggested by J. Chamberlain (1979), Barrows and Tamblyn (1980), and J. M. Brown (1980) and used in the innovative Alverno College approach (O'Brien and Doherty, 1979).

Some Specifics

Problem solving can be taught, and problem-solving skills can be improved and applied to other areas with considerable effectiveness. While none of these contentions is accepted by all, the evidence is mounting. Successful programs such as Guided Design at West Virginia University, the approaches taken at Alverno College and the McMaster Medical School, and the McMaster Problem-Solving (MPS) Program argue for the development of and the transferability of problem-solving skills from one subject to another (Resnick, 1987; Wales, 1979; Mentkowski and Doherty, 1984a, 1984b; Neufeld, Norman, Feightner, and Barrows, 1981; Bennett, Sackett, Haynes, Neufeld, Tugwell, and Roberts, 1987; and Woods, Marshall, and Hrymak, 1989).

How might we start? Teachers can use the evidence of the novices' experience versus that of the experts as guidelines to creating teaching and learning objectives and in choosing activities for use in the classroom. Teachers should be sensitive to how individual differences affect learning—why the way one person solves a problem may not make sense to someone else. Some students need to polish their translational skills so that they can accurately transfer a problem description into another form. For some situations, such as chemical structures and physics, Larkin (1983) and Voss (1985) have shown the importance of visual and spatial representations. We need to be patient, to give explicit suggestions about how to draw diagrams, and to encourage flexibility. For further help, I recommend Black's materials (1980), Stonewater's *Introduction* (1976), R. H. McKim's *Experiences in Visual Thinking* (1972), and R. Arnheim's *Visual Thinking* (1969).

Personal preference affects how we teach. Because I tend to visualize, my own favorite way of explaining theories may communicate effectively to only half the class. Hence, for the key concepts in our courses, we may need to work out and present explanations in visual, verbal, and symbolic modes.

Teachers should begin by developing their students' awareness of the thinking process. Students will then be able to describe what they are doing and monitor and compare their approaches with those of role models or experts. See Schoenfeld (1982) on the importance experts attach to monitoring as they solve tough problems. Indeed, in our McMaster four-year research program, about 90 percent of the explicit training the students received was designed to make them aware of the processes they were using (Woods, Crowe, Hoffman, and Wright, 1979). When students were asked to reflect on what they did and make comparisons with what other students had done, this relatively simple experience seemed to have a great effect. According to external evaluators, these students had developed good problem-solving skills. The observers wrote,

> it is noticeable to an outsider that [the students] are very articulate about their own styles of problem solving. They display the confidence of people who know their craft and can explain it to others. At the very least, they have experienced a successful exercise in consciousness raising.

A graduate of the program, S. Lieske (1983), described how she was able to apply what she learned in the program in the business world. Even students who are already highly successful problem solvers, however, need to be made aware of their own problem-solving processes. I recommend that teachers use the Whimbey pairs (1975) along with the Whimbey–Lochhead materials (1980, 1984). See Woods (1984c) for details about a two-to-four hour workshop on how to use the pairs and other materials. Alternatively, J. Stice (1982) offers a variation on the Whimbey–Lochhead approach.

Strategies

Next, teachers can give students a *strategy*—a series of three to ten mental phases one goes through as a problem is solved. Then, teachers should show how they use a strategy before asking students to use one as a framework for the problem solving done in class. Schoenfeld (1982) and Larkin (1975) have demonstrated that the use of such a strategy improves problem-solving skill in the context of mathematics and physics, respectively. Polya's strategy is probably the best known. Schoenfeld (1982) and Woods (1984c) extend Polya's strategy to incorporate attitudinal components and separate the phases in which all approach the task similarly from those phases affected by individual style. For example, the McMaster six-step strategy is as follows:

- Read the problem situation. Control your stress. Be motivated.
- Analyze the terms. Check for meaning. Separate the goals, constraints, criteria, and givens.
- Create the internal representation. Explore the situation.
- Plan.
- Do.
- Look back.

Many teachers and students express concern that they might not be choosing the "right" strategy. True, there are over 60 different strategies described in the literature, but they tend to repeat the same steps with different names. Eventually each student will develop an individual strategy; teachers only provide a catalyst to initiate that development. In the application of the strategy, teachers should help students understand the importance of the "exploration" stage at which they create "internal models" of given external problem situations, models that they connect to their own knowledge structures. Here, students play with ideas and ask "what-if" questions. They look for what is important in the situation, what assumptions they can make, and what representation is most valuable. They relate the stated goal to the criteria and the available resources and try to isolate the "real" problem.

This is the *crucial* step and the one in which experts spend the most time (Schoenfeld, 1982). Teachers should reassure students that it is OK to go up blind alleys; they should guide students in the use of subject-specific tacit information. In the classroom, teachers might venture to model their own problem-solving process for students, talking aloud through the solution of a problem. (Teachers should *not* use a problem they have posed for themselves and thought about before coming to class: That would produce a model of *exercise* solving, not *problem* solving.)

In the planning stage, teachers should model a "working backward" tactic. Larkin et al (1980) and Voss (1985) have shown that we work backward when we are faced with *problems*. When we complete *exercises*, we tend to work forward. Most instructors intuitively model the wrong tactic when they do sample problems in class, because for them the problems—already solved—are only exercises. W. A. Wickelgren (1974), Stonewater (1976), and D. L. Marples (1980) give explicit suggestions about the working backward tactic. (See Smith, page 69, for a different interpretation.)

Teachers should emphasize the "looking back" step in the strategy (Barrows and Tamblyn, 1980; Larkin et al, 1980; Larkin, 1982; Frazer, 1982). We should help our students suppress the enthusiasm of accomplishment long enough to focus on such questions as these: "Is the answer reasonable?" "What did I learn from this problem?" "How can I embed this experience in my episodic, subject-specific, problem-solving knowledge structures?" "What other problems can I solve now that I have had this experience?"

The Teacher's Role

Teachers should acquire confidence in their facilitation skills. Instructors or lecturers—by those very names—tend to see their roles primarily as one-way communicators of ideas. But for developing problem-solving skills in others, a workshop style is far more effective. The facilitator's role is to ask provocative questions and to provide open-ended experiences. Facilitators help students reflect on their experiences, monitor their progress, challenge their assumptions, raise issues that need to be taken into account, stimulate and encourage, and create and maintain a warm, safe atmosphere in which individuals will be willing to share without fear of ridicule. The facilitator is not an expert who has all the answers.

One might suppose, then, that the best facilitator would not be expert in the discipline being presented. Such a facilitator, however, would not know when the students were off-base or had misinterpreted information. This would be detrimental to the students' learning and to the teacher's morale. If teachers feel uneasy in this new role, they might try being a facilitator in someone else's class, with that person on hand to keep the proceedings on track technically. Here are some of the questions and comments a facilitator habitually uses:

—Hmm.
—I'm not sure that I follow you.
—Would you mind repeating that so that I can understand your approach?
—Let's collect some more ideas about this.
—Any other ideas?
—Are you sure? Can you check that?
—Why is that? How come?
—Why did you come to that conclusion?
—Do you agree with what was just said?
—If what you suggest is true, then how would you explain . . .?
—Have you considered . . .?
—Do you think you need to look that up?
—You seem unsure. Where could we find information to help clarify that?
—Are there other ways to examine this problem?
—What are some of the assumptions here [major, minor, hidden, etc.]?
—Why did you study this? Why was this work done?
—How can these inconsistencies be reconciled?
—Give me some concrete examples.
—Where does this new information lead?
—So what?

This list is drawn from my own works, as well as the suggestions of Barrows and Tamblyn (1980) and R. E. Sparks (1984). As resident experts-in-reserve, facilitators should respond to direct inquiries only when sure that students have exhausted their own logic, and facilitators' intervention will not deprive students of a profitable learning experience. The Whimbey-pair awareness activity (Woods, 1984a) is an excellent way for teachers to polish not only their own facilitating skills but also those of their students. The role of the listener in the Whimbey pair is very similar to that of a facilitator.

This review only summarizes suggestions from research in cognitive and educational psychology. The picture is not yet complete. Nevertheless, a challenging and fascinating task is defined well enough to lead to positive action in the classroom.

Resource Programs

Other ideas can be gleaned from the major resources and sample programs described next and summarized in table 4, which also notes their strengths and appropriateness to the high school level. Several of the programs have generated

Table 4: *Resources*

Program name	Time (hours)	Scope of explicit training (not *just* opportunity)	Appropriateness for high school science
Alverno College Program	Integrated throughout	Wide range	**1/2
Covington's Productive Thinking Program	20 to 60	Broad range	*1/2
Creative Problem Solving	24	Strategy creativity	***
De Bono's CORT	60	Strategy, broadening perspectives, analysis, creativity	**1/2
Feuerstein's Instrumental Enrichment	Not yet studied in detail		
Guided Design	30	Strategy, heuristics, analysis, decision making	***
Karplus	10	Reasoning, Piagetian learning	***
Kepner-Tregoe	60	Defining, strategy, decision making	*
Life-Skills Program	200	Wide range	**1/2
McMaster Problem-Solving Program	130 for full	Wide range	***
McMaster Medical School	Integrated throughout	Learning with explicit training from tutor	*
Reid's ACS Tapes	Not yet studied in detail		
Rubenstien's Patterns in Problem Solving	40	Strategy, heuristics, statistics, decision making	**
Whimbey-Lochhead	2 to 50	Carefulness, accuracy, analysis (including reasoning)	***

*** Very appropriate.   ** Appropriate.   * Ideas need work before use.

outstanding texts, which might also serve as the basis for course development. No single resource, however, covers all the key issues broadly.

The Whimbey-Lochhead approach (1980) is strong on building reasoning skills, confidence, awareness of the problem-solving process, and habits of carefulness and accuracy. E. de Bono's (1983) Cognitive Research Trust (CoRT) material effectively keeps students asking questions, broadening their perspectives, and developing their creativity. These are interesting basic starting materials; however, problem-solving skills are difficult to put into place, and I have found that additional materials need to be brought in or developed to supplement the CoRT program.

Resources to facilitate learning that center around Piaget's levels of learning and the "learning cycle" (see Fuller, 1982) include F. Collea's program called *Development of Reasoning in Science* (DORIS) (1978), and R. G. Fuller's ADAPT (1977). Karplus and associates' *Science Teaching and the Development of Reasoning* (1977) features separate workbooks in general science, chemistry, biology, and physics. *Learning How to Learn* (Novak and Gowin, 1984) is one of the most pertinent resources for helping students create knowledge structures.

Creative Problem Solving (CPS) emphasizes creativity and the use of a strategy. Individualized adaptations of this particular approach are fairly widespread. The *Creative Behavior Guidebook* (Parnes, 1967) and *Creative Problem Solving: A Basic Course* (Isaksen and Treffinger, 1985) are helpful starting points. The Creative Education Foundation holds an annual conference, which can increase any teacher's competence with CPS. D. Reid's 1978 self-paced audio tutorial, also based on CPS, is available from the American Chemical Society.

Guided Design, also called *Guided Decision Making,* is another well-developed approach that is easier than many to implement. Teachers should find out if the project material has been developed in their disciplines. This program focuses on the application of a strategy and the elements of decision making in the context of small group activities. It offers textbooks—*Guided Design* by C. E. Wales and R. A. Stager (1974) and *Professional Decision Making* by Wales, A. H. Nardi, and Stager (1986), along with other materials by Wales and Stager (1970, 1984)—as well as teacher-training aides, a newsletter, and a wide variety of problem-based activities that have been developed in different disciplines and for different levels. At the high school level, for example, some illustrative problems are why a house's lights sometimes fail, why a drinking bird dips its head, why gurgling and splashing occur when liquid is poured and whether they affect the time necessary to pour it, and what happens when a driver drinks alcohol.

The various life-skills programs, such as S. Conger's (1973) and R. E. Nelson and colleagues' (1978), offer valuable ideas for developing many of the components of problem solving; however, most teachers will want to modify these for their own courses. Some of the resources developed for college programs are appropriate for high school students as well. These include M. F. Rubinstein's *Patterns in Problem Solving* (1975) and the MPS Program (Woods, Crowe, Taylor, and Wood, 1984). The MPS Program offers individual units and teacher's guides for about 30 different component skills needed by effective problem solvers. The materials are being used at the high school level. The *Productive Thinking Program* (Covington, Crutchfield, and Olton, 1974), M. Lipman's *Philosophy for Children Program* (1974), and R. M. Feuerstein's *Instrumental Enrichment* (1985), however, are primarily for elementary school students. C. H. Kepner and B. B. Tregoe's approach (*The Rational Manager,* 1976) was developed for industry and management. Nonetheless, some ideas can be extracted from all of these programs for high school science courses.

Two institutions I know of—Alverno College and the McMaster Medical School—have integrated the teaching of problem solving throughout their whole curriculum. Both offer helpful annual workshops.

The approach at Alverno is most closely related to problem solving as it might be taught in high school programs. Alverno researchers identified eight sets of skills to be integrated and developed throughout the four years of college. These are skills in communication, analysis, problem solving, making value judgments, interacting with others, taking responsibility for the environment, being involved in the contemporary world, and responding aesthetically. For each skill, the researchers identified objectives and methods to develop competencies at six ascending levels of accomplishment. Then, they decided which of the existing subject courses could help develop these competencies and created evaluation criteria and milestone activities to allow the students to demonstrate competence in real world, content-independent problem situations. The Alverno program is a model for teaching problem solving (see Mentkowski and Doherty, 1984a, 1984b).

The McMaster Medical School program features very little explicit training in problem solving, but problem solving is an integral part of its approach. Skill in this area is a criterion for admission into the school. The program itself integrates small group activities, self-directed learning, self-evaluation, problem-based learning, and problem solving specific to clinical practice of the sort I call "interrupted process application." The student talks aloud for part of the physician/patient interaction; then the process is interrupted for a time-out, during which the student and tutor discuss what has occurred so far. When the process continues, another student takes up the dialogue. Awareness building and tutoring as role modeling are explicit aims of the McMaster program. Tutors act as facilitators, not founts of information. The problem-solving process dovetails into self-directed and problem-based learning activities. Although this approach has little to say directly about the explicit teaching of problem solving, it is noteworthy in the way it evaluates problem-solving skill and integrates a broad range of problem-oriented learning experiences. See V. R. Neufeld and Barrows (1974), and Barrows and Tamblyn (1980) for more information.

A summary of these major resources, written in the context of college science, appears in my column "PS Corner," which has appeared regularly in the *Journal of College Science Teaching* since late 1983. (See Woods, 1983—.) Other resources, especially pertinent at the elementary level, are reviewed in appendix A of B. K. Beyer's *Developing a Thinking Skills Program* (1988).

Books

From the more than 200 books that have been published about how to improve problem solving, the following are particularly useful. (A few have already been mentioned in the program descriptions above.) For

- hints or heuristics—Polya (1985), J. C. Jones (1970), and Schoenfeld (1980)
- awareness and analytical thinking—Whimbey and Lochhead (1980, 1984)
- creativity—S. J. Parnes (1967), J. L. Adams (1974), A. B. van Gundy, Jr. (1981), and de Bono (1983)
- decision making—Rubinstein (1975) and I. L. Janis and L. Mann (1977)
- fundamentals—Entwistle (1981), de Bono (1969), N. L. Gage and D. C. Berliner (1975), H. J. Klausmeier and W. Goodwin (1975), J. R. Hayes (1981), and A. Newell and H. A. Simon (1972)
- learning skills—Knowles (1975), Novak and D. B. Gowin (1984), and T. Buzan (1974)
- attitudinal and stress components—H. Selye (1974), Chamberlain (1979), and Perry (1970)

Possible Models for Teaching Programs

N. Whitman's 1983 review considers the intellectual foundations and definitions of problem solving and creativity and focuses on three uses for problem-solving education: as a medium for teaching students a specific subject, as a subject in itself, and as a skill to be acquired within a subject. Whitman's examples are all at the college level. Glaser (1984) also cites examples, but he is more concerned with classifying the major resource programs listed above than with making new courses and approaches possible. He bases his classification on whether the programs teach problem solving as a subject or as a skill in another subject domain. L. B. Resnick's book (1987) is also particularly noteworthy.

In general, the essential steps in teaching problem solving are the same in all disciplines. See box and Woods (1987). In the context of these basic steps, we can discuss several options for teaching the subject.

> 1. Introduce a concept or skill in problem solving: For example, cite the steps in a strategy, the characteristics of an expert's use of it, memorization and comprehension of it as a concept, and how it fits into the knowledge structure related to problem solving.
> 2. Provide opportunities to practice applying this concept (and to receive explicit feedback) in humorous, nontechnical situations, as most major resource program developers recommend (e.g., de Bono, Wales and Stager, Whimbey, and Woods).
> 3. Provide opportunities (with feedback) to apply this concept in technically rich situations, such as to *problems* in chemistry, physics, biology, or Earth science (not *exercises*).
> 4. Develop the student's confidence that s/he can apply the concept to professional, real world problems, the sort of open-ended problems that a working chemist, physicist, biologist, or Earth scientist might encounter.
> 5. Extend the application to coping with real world, everyday situations.

Teaching problem solving as a separate course. This option, where one course is created specifically to develop the skills, causes the least upheaval in the overall system. If, as usually happens, however, the other teachers teach as they always have, problem solving remains in its own airtight compartment. This, then, is the least desirable of all the options.

Few such courses have been reported at the high school level. At the college level, examples include courses based in Rubinstein's *Patterns in Problem Solving*, Sparks' course on "Inventive Reasoning," Hayes' course on "Cognitive Process: Theory and Practice," Whimbey's course on "Accuracy in Thinking," and the Engineering and Management Department's week-long short courses on "Problem Solving and Interpersonal Skills" (Woods, 1989). Other courses are described in various issues of the newsletter, *PS News* (Woods, 1979a).

Programs of this sort share the following characteristics:
- Each focuses on a relatively narrow set of problem-solving skills: Rubinstein on mathematical decision making and heuristics; Sparks on creativity; Hayes on the psychological underpinnings; and Whimbey on accuracy in thinking, reasoning, and analysis.
- All embed components 1 and 2 from the box above (concept and practice).
- All recognize the need to help students develop confidence in applying their skills beyond the confines of the course and use different approaches to include components 3, 4, or 5.

The educators who have designed these courses and those who teach them are alike concerned with applications in subsequent coursework. But unless other teachers are also aware of these skills and consciously reinforce them, there is likely to be little transfer of learning.

Teaching problem solving as a "unit" embedded in other science courses. This approach is probably the place to start. Teachers must anticipate certain difficulties, however. For example, the problem-solving content must be limited, but not too limited. Problem-solving skills are difficult for students to acquire: There is no quick fix. I recommend a minimum of two hours of workshop—all that some instructors can spare from a course's content requirements—for students to develop a beginning awareness of the problem-solving process.

For the greatest impact, the skills unit should be coordinated with other courses in the department, and other teachers should agree to reinforce it by using terms and strategies consistently and avoiding unnecessary repetition. For example, if a ninth-grade teacher introduces Whimbey's awareness activities and McMaster's six-step strategy, teachers in subsequent courses should use Whimbey pairs occasionally to explore problems or to create knowledge structures. Another teacher should not abruptly substitute Polya's four-step strategy simply because s/he likes it better.

Teachers should resist the temptation to neglect component 2 (see box), the use of humorous, everyday examples. The first two steps must be introduced, developed patiently, and then followed by the third. During the "look back" phase with which most component 3 strategies conclude, students and teachers should reflect on the problem-solving process and generate ideas for its application to other problem situations. Then, teachers can add enrichment through components 4 and 5.

Has embedding a unit into a science course been tried? Apart from the programs described earlier, little use has been reported formally. However, this approach has been widely discussed at recurring educators' conferences on teaching and thinking and has been put into practice successfully in a number of schools.

In the schools in Peel County, Ontario, D. Baker describes an effective use of the Whimbey-pair method combined with a board game, "Thumbs Up." The goal was to increase awareness of the thinking process in four different disciplines—mathematics, science, English, and social science. This activity was bridged into each discipline by analyzing portions of the subject texts. Consistent language, terminology, and an approach across disciplines illustrated the generic nature of problem solving. Two other Ontario teachers also report successful problem-solving practices in their classrooms. In the first hour of class, V. Weeks asks the students in his senior-level physics class in Oakville what problem solving is, why it is important, and what are some of the different approaches people can take to a given problem. In Waterdown, A. Thomson teaches her 11 and 12 year olds the McMaster 6-step strategy as a series of 6 "thinking rooms," each providing appropriate special focus and thinking tools.

In the Oakland School District, Pontiac, Michigan, in 1985, L. Motz arranged for 18 to 20 contact hours of inservice workshops based on the MPS program. Only a few problem-solving skills were targeted: awareness, use of a strategy, defining problems, and creativity. The emphasis was on having teachers experience and evaluate potential workshop materials. Quite a few of the teachers in the district have since introduced these activities—or modifications of them—into their courses. As Motz says, "If we lecture, the students don't become thinkers. To help students become problem identifiers and problem solvers, we need a change in teaching style and a focus on specific problem-solving skills" (1985).

Motz's approach has been adopted by several college science departments, notably the University of Florida, Purdue (see Wankat, 1983), the University of Michigan (Fogler, 1983), and Twente University (Mettes et al, 1980). At McMaster, four required courses embed problem solving explicitly into the Chemical Engineering Program. We teach in teams, with one teacher responsible for the course content and the other for the problem-solving components. Separate courses can be set up, but they must be corequisites. The problem-solving teacher can choose a skill, develop it with components 1 and 2, help the students apply the skill to the homework for their course material, and then bring in components 4 and 5 through specially developed problem-solving materials and real world situations. This approach allows more time for problem solving than the unit method and gives the problem-solving instructor the flexibility to move on to component 3 when the students are ready.

Teaching problem solving as an integral part of the science curriculum. Alverno's and McMaster's MPS programs have already been described.

Summary

Problem solving is a *timely, pertinent,* and *challenging* skill to teach:

> *timely,* because much research is now available to guide us,
> *pertinent,* because we all need its skills,
> *challenging,* because they are extremely difficult skills to develop in our students.

Teaching problem solving is made easier if we convert it into learning objectives such as those in the box above.

Cognitive and educational psychological research reminds us of the importance of the knowledge structures that our students create—or fail to create—when they learn science. The implications of this and other findings are that we should:

- start by developing our students' awareness of the mental processes they use to solve problems
- be confident that problem-solving strategies can be taught
- be sensitive to individual differences and preferences
- use the fundamentals of cognitive and attitudinal psychology to guide our understanding of problem solving as a subject and as a skill
- use novice-versus-expert research in the creation of learning objectives and the selection of activities to develop students' confidence and competence in their problem-solving abilities
- guide students in acquiring the tacit information of science
- encourage them to be active and use pencil and paper as they solve problems
- help them create an internal representation of the problem situation
- help them use the tactic of "working backward" as they devise a plan
- emphasize and provide practice in applying the "look back" stage
- introduce a variety of hints and heuristics and encourage students to select and apply the ones they prefer
- become comfortable in the role of facilitator and confidence builder

In short, we teachers must rise to meet the need to help students become problem solvers—a timely, pertinent, and challenging task we must tackle immediately.

References

Adams, J. L. (1974). *Conceptual blockbusting.* San Francisco: W. H. Freeman.

Arnheim, R. (1969). *Visual thinking.* Berkeley: University of California Press.

Ashmore, A. D., et al. (1979). Problem solving and problem solving networks in chemistry. *Journal of Chemical Education, 56,* 377-379.

Baker, D. (1989). Personal communication.

Barrows, H. S., and Tamblyn, R. M. (1980). *Problem-based learning: An approach to medical education.* New York: Springer.

Bhaskar, R., and Simon, H. (1970). Problem solving in semantically rich domains. *Cognitive Science, 1,* 195-215.

Black, P. J. (1980). Learning skills. In J. L. Lubkin (Ed.), *The teaching of elementary problem solving in engineering and related fields* (pp. 131-148). Washington, DC: American Society for Engineering Education.

Bennett, K. J., Sackett, D. L., Haynes, R. B., Neufeld, V. R., Tugwell, P., and Roberts, R. (1987). A controlled trial of teaching critical appraisal of the clinical literature to medical students. *Journal of the American Medical Association, 257*(18), 2451-2454.

Beyer, B. K. (1988). *Developing a thinking-skills program.* Boston: Allyn and Bacon.

Bloom, B. S., and Broder, L. J. (1950). *Problem solving processes of college students* (Supplementary Educational Monograph No. 73). Chicago: University of Chicago Press.

Bloom, B. S., et al. (1956). *Taxonomy of educational objectives: Cognitive domain.* New York: David McKay.

Boud, D., and Gray, T. G. F. (1978). Cultivation of professional engineering skills—Development of a tutorial method. *European Journal of Engineering Education, 3,* 117-133.

Brown, J. M. (1980). Learning skills as an overlay in elementary calculus. In J. L. Lubkin (Ed.), *The teaching of elementary problem solving in engineering and related fields* (pp. 115-130). Washington, DC: American Society for Engineering Education.

Burton, L. (1979). Personal communication.

Buzan, T. (1974). *Use your head.* London: British Broadcasting Corporation.

Caillot, M. (1983). Problem-solving research in elementary electricity. . . . *Problem Solving, 5*(3), 2.

Chamberlain, J. (1979). *Eliminating your self-defeating behaviors.* Provo, UT: Brigham Young University Press.

Chi, M. T. H., et al. (1981). Categorization and representation of physics problems by experts and novices. *Cognitive Science, 5,* 121-152.

Clement, J. (1978a). *Formula-centered knowledge versus conceptual understanding in physics.* (Tech. Rep.). Amherst, MA: University of Massachusetts, Department of Physics and Astronomy, Conceptual Development Project.

Clement, J. (1978b). *Cataloguing students' conceptual models in physics* (Final report to the National Science Foundation/RULE [Research in Undergraduate Learning Experience] Program). Amherst, MA: University of Massachusetts, Department of Physics and Astronomy.

Collea, F. (1978). *DORIS: Development of reasoning in science.* Fullerton, CA: California State University.

Conger, S. (1973). *Life skills coaching manual.* Available from Occupational and Career Analysis and Development Branch, Place de Portage, Phase VI, Ottawa, Ontario.

Covington, M. V., Crutchfield, R. S., and Olton, R. M., Jr. (1974). *Productive thinking program.* Columbus, OH: Charles E. Merrill.

Culver, R. S. (1987). Workshop: Rational curriculum design. In L. P. Grayson and J. M. Biedenbach (Eds.), *1987 Frontiers in Education Conference Proceedings* (pp. 391-396). Washington, DC: American Society for Engineering Education.

De Bono, E. (1967). *The uses of lateral thinking.* Hammondsworth, England: Pelican.

De Bono, E. (1969). *The mechanisms of the mind.* Hammondsworth, England: Pelican.

De Bono, E. (1983). *De Bono's thinking course.* London: British Broadcasting Corporation.

Entwistle, N. (1981). *Styles of learning and teaching.* New York: J. Wiley.

Eylon, B-S., and Reif, F. (1984). Effects of knowledge organization on task performance. *Cognition and Instruction, 1,* 5-44.

Feuerstein, R. (1985). *Instrumental enrichment.* Baltimore: University Park Press.*

Fisher, K. M., Lipson, J. I., Hildebrand, A. C., Miguel, L., Schoenberg, N., and Porter, N. (1986, February). Student misconceptions and teacher assumptions in biology. *Journal of College Science Teaching, 15*(4), 276-480.

---

*For further information, see Narrold, H., and Narrold, P. (1977), An introduction to Feuerstein's methods of assessing and actualizing cognitive potential, in S. Miezitis and M. Orme (Eds.), *Innovation in school psychology* (pp. 110-114). Toronto, Ontario: Ontario Institute for Studies in Education.

Fitch, P., and Culver, R. S. (1984). Educational activities to stimulate intellectual development in Perry's scheme. *1984 American Society for Engineering Education Annual Conference Proceedings* (pp. 712-717). Washington, DC: American Society for Engineering Education.

Fogler, H. S. (1983). The design of a course in problem solving. In J. T. Sears and R. K. Dean (Eds.), *Problem solving* (American Institute of Chemical Engineers Symposium Series No. 228) (pp. 40-49). New York: American Institute of Chemical Engineers.

Frazer, M. J. (1982). Solving chemical problems. *Chemical Society Review, 11,* 171.

Freeland, R. J., and Larkin, J. L. (1984). *Representation and problem solving: The role of elaboration.* Unpublished manuscript, Carnegie Mellon University, Department of Psychology, Pittsburgh.

Friedman, H. H. (1987). *Problem-oriented medical diagnosis.* Boston: Little, Brown.

Fuller, R. G. (1977). *ADAPT.* Lincoln, NE: University of Nebraska.

Fuller, R. G. (1982). *Piagetian programs in higher education.* Lincoln, NE: University of Nebraska.

Gage, N. L., and Berliner, D. C. (1975). *Educational psychology* (2nd ed.). Chicago: Rand McNally.

Glaser, R. (1984). Education and thinking: The role of knowledge. *American Psychologist, 39*(2), 93-104.

Gold, V., Kershaw, M. J., and Millen, D. J. (1980). Skills required at A-level. *Education in Chemistry, 17,* 170-171.

Greenfield, L. B. (1979). Engineering student problem solving. In J. Lochhead and J. Clement (Eds.), *Cognitive process instruction* (pp. 229-238). Philadelphia: Franklin Institute.*

Greenfield, L. B. (1980). Engineering student problem solving. In J. L. Lubkin (Ed.), *The teaching of elementary problem solving in engineering and related fields* (pp. 87-96). Washington, DC: American Society for Engineering Education.*

Harrisberger, L., Heydinger, R., Seeley, J., and Talburtt, M. (1976). *Experiential learning in engineering education.* Washington, DC: American Society for Engineering Education.

Hayes, J. R. (1981). *The complete problem solver.* Philadelphia: Franklin Institute.

Helm, H. (1980). Misconceptions in physics amongst South African students. *Physics Education, 18,* 92-97.

Heppner, P. P., et al. (1982). Personal problem solving: A descriptive study of individual differences. *Journal of Counseling Psychology, 29,* 580-590.

Isaksen, S. G., and Treffinger, D. J. (1985). *Creative problem solving: The basic course.* Buffalo, NY: Bearly.

Janis, I. L., and Mann, L. (1977). *Decision making.* New York: MacMillan, Free Press.

Jones, J. C. (1970). *Design methods.* New York: Wiley Interscience.

Karplus, R., et al. (1977). *Science teaching and the development of reasoning.* Berkeley, CA: Lawrence Hall of Science. (The series includes books in general science, chemistry, biology, and physics.)

Kepner, C. H., and Tregoe, B. B. (1976). *The rational manager.* Princeton, NJ: Authors. (Originally published 1965 by McGraw-Hill)

Klausmeier, H. J., and Goodwin, W. (1972). *Learning and human abilities: Educational psychology* (4th ed.). New York: Harper and Row.

Knowles, M. (1975). *Self-directed learning.* Chicago: Follett.

Larkin, J. H. (1975). *Developing useful instruction in thinking skills.* Unpublished manuscript, Department of Physics, University of California, Berkeley.†

Larkin, J. H. (1979a). Information-processing models and science instruction. In J. Lochhead and J. Clement (Eds.), *Cognitive process instruction* (pp. 109-118). Philadelphia: Franklin Institute.

Larkin, J. H. (1979b). Processing information for effective problem solving. *Engineering Education, 70,* 285-288.

Larkin, J. H. (1980). Teaching problem solving in physics: The psychological laboratory and the practical classroom. In D. T. Tuma and R. Reif (Eds.), *Problem solving and education: Issues in teaching and research* (pp. 111-125). Hillsdale, NJ: Erlbaum.

Larkin, J. H. (1982). *The cognition of learning physics.* Unpublished manuscript, Carnegie Mellon University, Department of Psychology, Pittsburgh.

Larkin, J. H. (1983). *Spatial reasoning in solving physics problems.* Unpublished manuscript, Carnegie Mellon University, Department of Psychology, Pittsburgh.

---

*While these two Greenfield papers are identically titled, their content differs slightly.

†See also Larkin's other unpublished papers in this series (1976, 1977a, 1977b, 1977c), all at the University of California, Berkeley.

Larkin, J. H., and Reif, F. (1979). Understanding and teaching problem solving in physics. *European Journal of Science Education, 1,* 191–203.

Larkin, J. H., et al. (1980). Expert and novice performance in solving physics problems. *Science, 208,* 1335–1342.

Lewis, R. (1982). Theories, structure, teaching, and learning. *Bioscience, 32*(9), 734–737.

Lieske, S. (1983). Problem solving in industry. In J. T. Sears and R. K. Dean (Eds.), *Problem solving* (American Institute of Chemical Engineers Symposium Series No. 228) (pp. 54–56). New York: American Institute of Chemical Engineers.

Lin, H. S. (1979a). Problem solving in introductory physics: Demons and difficulties (Doctoral dissertation, Massachusetts Institute of Technology). *Dissertation Abstracts International, 39.* (University Microfilms No. AAC0348163)

Lin, H. S. (1979b). The hidden curriculum of the introductory physics classroom. *Engineering Education, 70,* 289–294.

Lipman, M. (1974). *Philosophy for children program.* Montclair College, Institute for the Advancement of Philosophy for Children, Montclair, NJ.

Lochhead, J., and Clement, J. (Eds.). (1979). *Cognitive process instruction.* Philadelphia: Franklin Institute.

Marples, D. L. (1980). A backwards-reasoning model of problem solving. In J. L. Lubkin (Ed.), *The teaching of elementary problem solving in engineering and related fields* (pp. 97–114). Washington, DC: American Society for Engineering Education.

McCaulley, M. H., et al. (1983). Applications of psychological type in engineering education. *Engineering Education, 73*(5), 394–400.

McKim, R. H. (1980). *Experiences in visual thinking* (2nd ed.). Monterey, CA: Brooks/Cole.

Mentkowski, M., and Doherty, A. (1984a). Abilities that last a lifetime: Outcomes of the Alverno experience. *American Association of Higher Education Bulletin, 36,* 5–14.

Mentkowski, M., and Doherty, A. (1984b). *Careering after college.* (Final report to the National Institute of Education). Alverno College, Milwaukee.

Mettes, C. T. C. W., et al. (1980). Teaching and learning problem solving in science. *Journal of Chemical Education 57*(12), 882–885 and *58*(1), 51–55.

Nelson, R. E., et al. (1978). *Methods and materials for teaching occupational survival skills.* Curriculum Clearing House, Illinois State Board of Education. Macomb, IL: Western Illinois University.

Neufeld, V. R., and Barrows, H. S. (1974). *The McMaster philosophy: An approach to medical education* (Educational Monograph No. 5). McMaster University Faculty of Medicine, Hamilton, Ontario.

Neufeld, V. R., Norman, G. R., Feightner, J. W., and Barrows, H. S. (1981). Clinical problem solving by medical students: A cross-sectional and longitudinal analysis. *Medical Education, 15,* 315–322.

Newell, A., and Simon, H. A. (1972). *Human problem solving.* Englewood Cliffs, NJ: Prentice-Hall.

Novak, J. D. (1984). Application of advances in learning theory and philosophy of science to the improvement of chemistry teaching. *Journal of Chemical Education, 61,* 607–612.

Novak, J. D. (1989). The role of content and process in the education of science teachers. In P. F. Brandwein and A. H. Passow (Eds.), *Gifted young in science: Potential through performance* (pp. 307–320). Washington, DC: NSTA.

Novak, J. D., and Gowin, D. B. (1984). *Learning how to learn.* New York: Cambridge University Press.

O'Brien, K., and Doherty, A. (1979). Personal communication.

Ogborn, J. (1977). *Small group teaching in undergraduate science.* London: Heinemann Educational Books.

Parnes, S. J. (1967). *Creative behavior guidebook.* New York: Charles Scribner.

Perry, W. G., Jr. (1970). *Forms of intellectual and ethical behavior in the college years.* New York: Holt, Rinehart, and Winston.

Polya, G. (1985). *How to solve it* (2nd ed.). New York: Macmillan.

The problem of problem solving. (1982). *Problem Solving, 4*(9), 1.

Reid, D. (1978). *Applied problem solving through creative thinking.* Washington, DC: American Chemical Society.

Reif, F. (1982a). *Making scientific concepts and principles effectively usable: Requisite knowledge and teaching implications.* Unpublished manuscript, University of California, Department of Physics, Berkeley.

Reif, F. (1982b). *Cognitive processes facilitating scientific problem solving: Some systematic studies and educational implications.* Unpublished manuscript, University of California, Department of Physics, Berkeley.

Reif, F., and Heller, J. J. (1982). *Knowledge structures and problem solving in physics.* Unpublished manuscript, University of California, Department of Physics, Berkeley.

Reif, F., et al. (1976). Teaching general learning and problem-solving skills. *American Journal of Physics, 44,* 212–217.

Resnick, L. B. (1987). *Education and learning to think.* Washington, DC: National Academy Press.

Rubinstein, M. F. (1975). *Patterns in problem solving.* Englewood Cliffs, NJ: Prentice Hall.

Schoenfeld, A. H. (1979a). Can heuristics be taught? In J. Lochhead and J. Clement (Eds.), *Cognitive process instruction* (pp. 315–338). Philadelphia: Franklin Institute.

Schoenfeld, A. H. (1979b). Explicit heuristic training as a variable in problem-solving performance. *Journal for Research in Math Education, 10,* 173–187.

Schoenfeld, A. H. (1979c). *Teaching mathematical problem-solving skills.* Unpublished paper, Hamilton College, Department of Mathematics, Clinton, NY.

Schoenfeld, A. H. (1980). Heuristics in the classroom. In S. Krulick (Ed.), *Problem solving in school mathematics* [1980 Yearbook of the National Council of Teachers of Mathematics] (pp. 9–22). Reston, VA: National Council of Teachers of Mathematics.

Schoenfeld, A. H. (1982). Episodes and executive decisions in mathematical problem solving. In R. Lesh and M. Landau (Eds.), *Acquisition of mathematical concepts and processes* (pp. 345–395). New York: Academic Press.

Schoenfeld, A. H., and Herrmann, D. J. (1981). *Problem perception and knowledge structure in expert and novice mathematical problem solvers.* Unpublished manuscript, University of Rochester, Department of Mathematics, Rochester, NY.

Selvaratnam, M. (1983). Students' mistakes in problem solving. *Education in Chemistry, 20,* 125–132.

Selye, H. (1974). *Stress without distress.* Toronto, Ontario: McClelland Steward.

Sloan, E. D. (1982). An experiential design course in groups. *Chemical Engineering Education, 16,* 38–41.

Sloan, E. D., and Jens, K. S. (1982). Differences and implications in faculty and student types on the Myers-Briggs type indicator. *1982 American Society for Engineering Education Annual Conference Proceedings* (pp. 168–171). Washington, DC: American Society for Engineering Education.

Smith, M. U. (1988). Successful and unsuccessful problem solving in classical genetic pedigrees. *Journal of Research in Science Teaching, 25,* 411–433.

Smith, M. U., and Good, R. (1984). Problem solving and classical genetics: Successful versus unsuccessful performance. *Journal of Research in Science Teaching, 21,* 895–912.

Smith, P. (1981). *The development of a taxonomy of the life skills required to become a balanced, self-determined person.* Ottawa and Ontario: Occupational and Career Analysis and Development Branch, Employment and Immigration.

Sparks, R. E. (1984). Personal communication.

Stice, J. (1982, May). Teaching problem-solving skills. *Education Society Institute of Electrical and Electronics, Inc./American Society for Engineering Education Newsletter,* pp. 16–17.

Stonewater, J. K. (1976). *Introduction to reasoning and problem solving.* Unpublished manuscript, Michigan State University, East Lansing.

Thomson, A. (1989). Personal communication.

Torrance, E. P. (1979). *The search for satori and creativity.* Buffalo, NY: Creative Education Foundation.

Trowbridge, D. E., and McDermott, L. C. (1980, December). An investigation of student understanding of the concept of velocity in one dimension. *American Journal of Physics, 48*(12), 1020–1028.

Trowbridge, D. E., and McDermott, L. C. (1981, March). An investigation of student understanding of the concept of acceleration in one dimension. *American Journal of Physics, 49*(3), 242–253.

Van Gundy, A. B., Jr. (1981). *Techniques of structured problem solving.* New York: Van Nostrand Reinhold.

Voss, J. F. (1985). Problem solving and the educational process. In R. Glaser and A. Lesgold (Eds.), *Handbook of psychology and education* (pp. 251–294). Hillsdale, NJ: Erlbaum.

Waldrop, M. M. (1984). The necessity of knowledge. *Science, 223,* 1279–1282.

Wales, C. E. (1979). Does how you teach make a difference? *Engineering Education, 69,* 394–398.

Wales, C. E., Nardi, A. H., and Stager, R. A. (1986). *Professional decision making.* Morgantown, WV: West Virginia University, Center for Guided Design.

Wales, C. E., and Stager, R. A. (1970). *Education systems design.* Unpublished manuscript, West Virginia University, Center for Guided Design, Morgantown.

Wales, C. E., and Stager, R. A. (1974). *Guided design.* St. Paul, MN: West Publishing.

Wales, C. E., and Stager, R. A. (1984). *Successful decision making.* Unpublished manuscript, West Virginia University, Center for Guided Design, Morgantown.

Wankat, P. C. (1983). Analysis of student mistakes and improvement of problem solving on McCabe-Thiele binary distillation tests. In J. T. Sears and R. K. Dean (Eds.),

Problem solving (American Institute of Chemical Engineers Symposium Series No. 228) (pp. 33–39). New York: American Institute of Chemical Engineers.

Weeks, V. (1989). Personal communication.

Whimbey, A. (1975). Personal communication.

Whimbey, A., and Lochhead, J. (1980). *Problem solving and comprehension.* Philadelphia: Franklin Institute.

Whimbey, A., and Lochhead, J. (1984). *Beyond problem solving.* Philadelphia: Franklin Institute.

Whitman, N. (1983). Teaching problem solving and creativity in college courses. *American Association of Higher Education Bulletin, 35*(9), 9–13.

Wickelgren, W. A. (1974). *How to solve problems: Elements of a theory of problems and problem solving.* San Francisco: Freeman.

Woods, D. R. (1979a—). *PS news.* Newsletter.

Woods, D. R. (1979b). Teaching problem-solving skills. *Conference Proceedings of Frontiers in Education* (pp. 293–297). Washington, DC: American Society of Engineering Education.

Woods, D. R. (Contributing Ed.). (1983—). PS corner. *Journal of College Science Teaching, 13—*

    13, [1983] September/October (1), 53–56; November (2), 112–113; [1983–1984] December/ January (3), 182–184; [1984] February (4), 319–322; March/April (5), 380–383; May (6), 467–472.

    14, [1984] September/October (1), 68–71; November (2), 134–136; [1984–1985] December/ January (3), 204–206; [1985] February (4), 352–353; March/April (5), 444–446; May (6), 522–525.

    15, [1985] September/October (1), 62–64; November (2), 148–150; [1985–1986] December/January (3), 212–215; [1986] February (4), 409–412; March/April (5), 486–490; May (6), 550–554.

    16, [1986] September/October (1), 68–72; November (2), 127–130; [1986–1987] December/January (3), 212–217; [1987] February (4), 384–389; March/April (5), 480–484; May (6), 565–568, 570.

    17, [1987] November (2), 166–172; [1987–1988] December/January (3), 241–243; [1988] February (4), 317–321; March/April (5), 401–403.

    18, [1988] September/October (1), 77–79, 66–67; November (2), 138–141; [1988–1989] December/January (3), 193–195; [1989] February (4), 259–261; March/April (5), 338–340.

Woods, D. R. (1983a). Introducing explicit training in problem solving into our courses. *HERD [Higher Education Research Development], 2*(1), 79–102.

Woods, D. R. (1983b). Introducing tacit information. *Problem Solving, 5,* 1.

Woods, D. R. (1983c, September/October). PS corner. *Journal of College Science Teaching, 13*(1), 53–56.

Woods, D. R. (1984a, May). PS corner. *Journal of College Science Teaching, 13*(6), 467–472.

Woods, D. R. (1984b). *Skills for problem solving.* Unpublished manuscript, McMaster University, Hamilton, Ontario.

Woods, D. R. (1984c). *Strategy for problem solving.* Unpublished manuscript, McMaster University, Hamilton, Ontario.

Woods, D. R. (1987). How might I teach problem solving? In J. E. Stice (Ed.), *New directions in teaching and learning: Developing critical-thinking and problem-solving abilities* (No. 30) (pp. 55–71). San Francisco: Jossey-Bass.

Woods, D. R. (1989). *Problem solving and interpersonal skills program 1.* Unpublished manuscript, McMaster University, Department of Engineering and Management, Hamilton, Ontario.

Woods, D. R., and Crowe, C. M. (1984). Characteristics of engineering students in their first two years. *Engineering Education, 73*(5), 289–295.

Woods, D. R., Crowe, C. M., Hoffman, T. W., Wright, J. D. (1979). Major challenges to teaching problem solving. *Engineering Education, 70*(3), 277–284.

Woods, D. R., Crowe, C. M., Hoffman, T. W., and Wright, J. D. (1985). Fifty-six challenges to teaching problem-solving skills, *Chem 13 News, 155,* 1–12.

Woods, D. R., Crowe, C. M., Taylor, P. A., and Wood, P. E. (1984). The MPS program. *Proceedings of the 1984 American Society for Engineering Education Annual Conference* (pp. 1021–1035). Washington, DC: American Society for Engineering Education.

Woods, D. R., Marshall, R. R., and Hrymak, A. N. (1989). *Outcomes of the MPS Program* [internal report]. Hamilton, Ontario: McMaster University.

Woods, D. R., Wright, J. D., Hoffman, T. W., Swartman, R. K., Doig, I. D. (1975). Teaching problem-solving skills. *Annals of Engineering Education, 1*(1), 239–243.

Yokomoto, C. F., and Ware, J. R. (1982). Improving problem-solving performance using MBTI. *Proceedings of the American Society for Engineering Education Annual Conference* (pp. 163–167). Washington, DC: American Society for Engineering Education.